CCNP Security - SITCS
Exam (300-210)

Technology Workbook

Implementing Cisco Threat Control Solutions (SITCS)
Associated Certification: CCNP Security

www.ipspecialist.net

Document Control

Proposal Name	:	SITCS Workbook
Document Version	:	1.0
Document Release Date	:	18-Sep-19
Reference	:	CCNP_Security_WorkBook

Feedback:

If you have any comments regarding the quality of this book, or otherwise alter it to better suit your needs, you can contact us through email at info@ipspecialist.net

Please make sure to include the book's title and ISBN in your message.

About IPSpecialist

IPSPECIALIST LTD. IS COMMITTED TO EXCELLENCE AND DEDICATED TO YOUR SUCCESS.

Our philosophy is to treat our customers like family. We want you to succeed, and we are willing to do everything possible to help you make it happen. We have the proof to back up our claims. We strive to accelerate billions of careers with great courses, accessibility, and affordability. We believe that continuous learning and knowledge evolution are the most important things to keep re-skilling and up-skilling the world.

Planning and creating a specific goal is where IPSpecialist helps. We can create a career track that suits your visions as well as develop the competencies you need to become a professional Network Engineer. We can also assist you with the execution and evaluation of your proficiency level, based on the career track you choose, as they are customized to fit your specific goals.

We help you STAND OUT from the crowd through our detailed IP training content packages.

Course Features:

❖ Self-Paced Learning
  ● Learn at your own pace and in your own time
❖ Covers Complete Exam Blueprint
  ● Prep-up for the exam with confidence
❖ Case Study Based Learning
  ● Relate the content with real-life scenarios
❖ Subscriptions that suits you
  ● Get more and pay less with IPS subscriptions
❖ Career Advisory Services
  ● Let the industry experts plan your career journey
❖ Virtual Labs to test your skills
  ● With IPS vRacks, you can evaluate your exam preparations
❖ Practice Questions
  ● Practice Questions to measure your preparation standards
❖ On Request Digital Certification
  ● On request digital certification from IPSpecialist LTD.

About the Authors:

This book has been compiled with the help of multiple professional engineers. These engineers specialize in different fields e.g. Networking, Security, Cloud, Big Data, IoT etc. Each engineer develops content in his/her own specialized field that is compiled to form a comprehensive certification guide.

About the Technical Reviewers:

Nouman Ahmed Khan

AWS-Architect, CCDE, CCIEX5 (R&S, SP, Security, DC, Wireless), CISSP, CISA, CISM, Nouman Ahmed Khan is a Solution Architect working with a major telecommunication provider in Qatar. He works with enterprises, mega-projects, and service providers to help them select the best-fit technology solutions. He also works as a consultant to understand customer business processes and helps select an appropriate technology strategy to support business goals. He has more than fourteen years of experience working in Pakistan/Middle-East & UK. He holds a Bachelor of Engineering Degree from NED University, Pakistan, and M.Sc. in Computer Networks from the UK.

Abubakar Saeed

Abubakar Saeed has more than twenty-five years of experience, managing, consulting, designing, and implementing large-scale technology projects, extensive experience heading ISP operations, solutions integration, heading Product Development, Pre-sales, and Solution Design. Emphasizing on adhering to Project timelines and delivering as per customer expectations, he always leads the project in the right direction with his innovative ideas and excellent management skills.

Muhammad Yousuf

Muhammad Yousuf is a professional technical content writer. He is a Certified Ethical Hacker (v10) and Cisco Certified Network Associate in Routing and Switching, holding a Bachelor's Degree in Telecommunication Engineering from Sir Syed University of Engineering and Technology. He has both technical knowledge and industry sounding information, which he uses perfectly in his career.

Free Resources:

With each workbook bought from Amazon, IPSpecialist offers free resources to our valuable customers.

Once you buy this book, you will have to contact us at support@ipspecialist.net or tweet @ipspecialistnet to get this limited time offer without any extra charges.

Free Resources Include:

Exam Practice Questions in Quiz Simulation: With more than 300+ Q/A, IPSpecialist's Practice Questions is a concise collection of important topics to keep in mind. The questions are especially prepared following the exam blueprint to give you a clear understanding of what to expect from the certification exam. It goes further on to give answers with thorough explanations. In short, it is a perfect resource that helps you evaluate your preparation for the exam.

Career Report: This report is a step by step guide for a novice who wants to develop his/her career in the field of computer networks. It answers the following queries:

- What are the current scenarios and future prospects?
- Is this industry moving towards saturation or are new opportunities knocking at the door?
- What will the monetary benefits be?
- Why to get certified?
- How to plan and when will I complete the certifications if I start today?
- Is there any career track that I can follow to accomplish specialization level?

Furthermore, this guide provides a comprehensive career path towards being a specialist in the field of networking and also highlights the tracks needed to obtain certification.

IPS Personalized Technical Support for Customers: Good customer service means helping customers efficiently, in a friendly manner. It is essential to be able to handle issues for customers and do your best to ensure they are satisfied. Providing good service is one of the most important things that can set our business apart from the others of its kind.

Great customer service will result in attracting more customers and attain maximum customer retention.

IPS is offering personalized TECH support to its customers to provide better value for money. If you have any queries related to technology and labs, you can simply ask our technical team for assistance via Live Chat or Email.

Our Products

Technology Workbooks
IPSpecialist Technology workbooks are the ideal guides to developing the hands-on skills necessary to pass the exam. Our workbooks cover official exam blueprint and explain the technology with real life case study based labs. The contents covered in each workbook consist of individually focused technology topics presented in an easy-to-follow, goal-oriented, step-by-step approach. Every scenario features detailed breakdowns and thorough verifications to help you completely understand the task and associated technology.

We extensively used mind maps in our workbooks to visually explain the technology. Our workbooks have become a widely used tool to learn and remember the information effectively.

vRacks
Our highly scalable and innovative virtualized lab platforms let you practice the IP Specialist Technology Workbook at your own time and your own place as per your convenience.

Quick Reference Sheets
Our quick reference sheets are a concise bundling of condensed notes of the complete exam blueprint. It is an ideal and handy document to help you remember the most important technology concepts related to the certification exam.

Practice Questions
IP Specialists' Practice Questions are dedicatedly designed from a certification exam perspective. The collection of these questions from our technology workbooks are prepared keeping the exam blueprint in mind covering not only important but necessary topics as well. It is an ideal document to practice and revise for your certification.

Table of Contents

About this Workbook

This workbook covers all the information you need to pass the Implementing Cisco Threat Control Solutions 300-210 exam. The workbook is designed to take a practical approach of learning with real life examples and case studies.

- ➢ Covers complete Route blueprint
- ➢ Summarized content
- ➢ Case Study based approach

- ➢ Ready to practice labs on vRacks
- ➢ Pass guarantee
- ➢ Mind maps

Cisco Certifications

Cisco Systems, Inc. is a global technology leader, specializing in networking and communications products and services. The company is probably best known for its business routing and switching products, which direct data, voice and video traffic across networks around the world.

Cisco offers one of the most comprehensive vendor-specific certification programs in the world. The Cisco Career Certification program begins at the Entry level, then advances to Associate, Professional and Expert levels, and (for some certifications) caps things off at the Architect level.

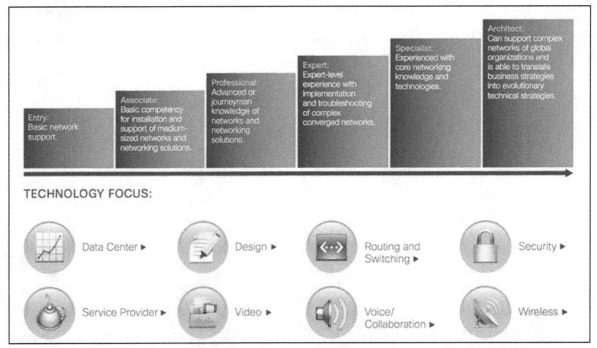

Figure 1 Cisco Certifications Skill Matrix

How does Cisco certifications help?

Cisco certifications are a de facto standard in networking industry help you boost your career in the following ways:

1. Gets your foot in the door
2. Screen job applicants
3. Validate the technical skills of the candidate
4. Ensure quality, competency, and relevancy
5. Improves organization credibility and customer's loyalty
6. Required to maintain organization partnership level with OEMs
7. Helps in Job retention and promotion
8. Boosts your confidence level

Cisco Certification Tracks

Certification Tracks	Entry	Associate	Professional	Expert	Architect
Collaboration				CCIE Collaboration	
Data Center		CCNA Data Center	CCNP Data Center	CCIE Data Center	
Design	CCENT	CCDA	CCDP	CCDE	CCAr
Routing & Switching	CCENT	CCNA Routing and Switching	CCNP	CCIE Routing & Switching	
Security	CCENT	CCNA Security	CCNP Security	CCIE Security	
Service Provider		CCNA Service Provider	CCNP Service Provider	CCIE Service Provider	
Service Provider Operations	CCENT	CCNA Service Provider Operations	CCNP Service Provider Operations	CCIE Service Provider Operations	
Video		CCNA Video			
Voice	CCENT	CCNA Voice	CCNP Voice	CCIE Voice	
Wireless	CCENT	CCNA Wireless	CCNP Wireless	CCIE Wireless	

Figure 2 Cisco Certifications Track

About the SITCS Exam

- ➢ **Exam Number:** 300-210
- ➢ **Associated Certifications:** CCNP_Security
- ➢ **Duration:** 90 minutes (65-75 questions)
- ➢ **Exam Registration:** Pearson VUE

The Implementing Cisco Threat Control Solutions (SITCS) exam (300-210) is part of the CCNP Security certification. It tests a network security engineer on advanced firewall architecture and configuration with the Cisco next-generation firewall, utilizing access and identity policies. This new revision of the SITCS exam replaces 300-207, removes some older technologies, and adds coverage for both Cisco Firepower NGIPS and Cisco AMP (Advanced Malware Protection). This 90-minute exam is consists of 65–75 questions and covers integration of Intrusion Prevention System (IPS) and context-aware firewall components, as well as Web (Cloud) and Email Security solutions. Candidates can prepare for this exam by taking the Implementing Cisco Threat Control Solutions (SITCS) course.

The following topics are general guidelines for the content likely to be included on the exam. However, other related topics may also appear on any specific delivery of the exam. In order to better reflect the contents of the exam and for clarity purposes, the guidelines below may change at any time without notice.

- ➢ Content Security   27%
- ➢ Network Threat Defense   22%
- ➢ Cisco FirePOWER Next-Generation IPS (NGIPS)   20%
- ➢ Security Architectures   17%
- ➢ Troubleshooting, Monitoring, and Reporting Tools   14%

Prerequisites

Valid Cisco CCNA Routing and Switching certification or any Cisco CCIE certification can act as a prerequisite.

How much an exam cost?

Computer-based certification exam (written exam) prices depend on scope and exam length. Please refer to the "Exam Pricing" webpage for details.

Step4: Getting the Results

After you complete an exam at an authorized testing centre, you'll get immediate online notification of your pass or fail status, a printed examination score report that indicates your pass or fail status, and your exam results by section.

Congratulations! You are now SITCS- Certified.

Chapter 1: Content Security

Cisco Cloud Web Security (CWS)

Using internet services from any company or office's internet connection or through any public internet services like the Public Wi-Fi at coffee shops or hotels is quite risky in terms of security and in keeping your system, files, and secret data and other information secure and safe. There might be any website waiting for you with harmful executable codes and scripts. In the Internet, there are many websites that contain malicious executable codes, harmful, and infected files and many more type of malicious things and malwares which you really don't want to destroy your system and files. These harmful materials can be auto-downloaded on your system or just waiting for your click before infecting your file. These infections can be spread by using harmful websites, pop-ups, advertisements and redirection to other websites. These can be targeted attacks or spread publically to gain access to the device of the user.

These web attacks and increasing malicious and malware infection through the internet are increasing day by day. As these attacks are increasing, it is becoming more important and necessary for IT to create some significant steps to prevent these unwanted activities. The number of cases infected by malwares and malicious traffic from websites are increasing, hence, costing in millions of dollars. Cisco offers Security devices for defense from these infections, which are Cisco Cloud Web Security (CWS) which is formerly known as Cisco ScanSafe as well as Cisco Web Security Appliance (WSA). These devices have become an integral Security Solution of IT for cloud and Web Security.

Cisco offers two security solutions for preventing these malwares and malicious traffic affecting the network resources. Cisco Web Security Appliance (WSA) which is more appropriate for a private network security. Endpoint stations accessing the network through a wired or wireless link or connecting remotely through a VPN, if these End stations are infected, this infection will be spread through all over the network. This is the prime objective to secure these End Stations from spreading malwares into the network and network devices. For these type of Private network, Cisco offers its Web Security Appliance which is discussed later in detail.

User and Endpoint stations are not connected through a direct link to the network or they are not always connected to the private network cloud. They may also be accessing the public Internet for entertainment, browsing and searching or for any other reason. When a user is accessing the public internet through a publically-available access such as a Public Wi-Fi service or from the Internet Cafe instead of connecting through a secure network, there is a higher chance that the User's PC or device can be infected and attacked by any malware, virus, or other attacks. These attacks can be costly in terms of disconnection,

disruption of activity, encryption of data and file and spreading of this infection to another network. For these type of networks, Cisco offers Cisco Cloud Web Security (CWS) to protect End Stations and Users devices from infection.

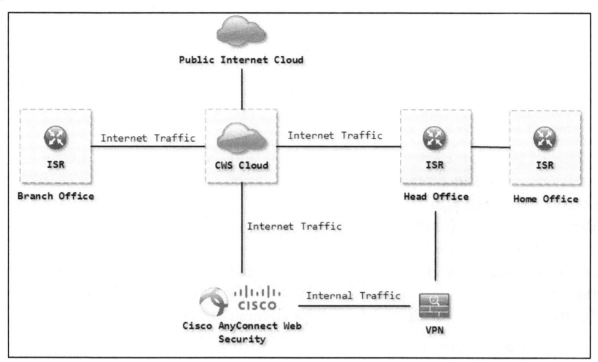

Figure 1-1: Cisco Cloud Web Security (CWS)

Cisco Cloud Web Security (CWS) depends upon three major components:

1. **Cisco Any Connect Client**

   Cisco AnyConnect Client application is for user end for every individual user for accessing the network.

2. **Cisco Cloud Web Security Cloud**

   CWS cloud is hosted in datacentre.

3. **Cisco Web Security Database**

   CWS Database is for reporting and logging purpose.

Features and Benefits of Cloud Web Security

Malware Prevention and Protection:

Prevention from malwares help limit data loss, information theft, and other unwanted activities from your device. Real-Time Web Protection by heuristics engines, Signature and other resources including granular visibility and Control of several thousands of applications at a time. billions of Web request can be processed and analyzed daily to detect, prevent and protect and defend against Web-based Threats.

Combined Integrated Solution

Combined Solution of Cisco Cloud Web Security (CWS) and Cisco Web Security Appliance (WSA) offers Malware protection and prevention from Public internet and infected User Endpoints infecting your corporate Network. It can also be integrated with Advanced Malware Protection (AMP) and Cognitive Threat Analytics (CTA). These devices in combined integration offers more visibility, effective controlling and intelligence and defense from malwares. This next level security integration protects from advanced threats. This security solution also offers identification of type and severity of these web based threats to take action, prioritize and protect from these attacks.

Centralized Management and Mobility:

Cisco Cloud Web Security CWS offers Centralized management for protecting your corporate network and devices supporting Mobility. User can connect remotely or directly to the network hence Cisco Web Security Solution supports remote and mobile users.

Policies Enforcement:

As Cisco AnyConnect Client and Cisco Integrated Services G2 Router automatically forward internet traffic to the data centre hosting Cisco Cloud Web Security Cloud which controls, monitors the Web traffic. Cisco CWS provides Monitoring and Controlling, Visibility and Reporting of Web traffics as well as Visibility of Malwares or unwanted malicious activities respect to the Policies configured for user access to Secure and Unsecure and harmful Websites.

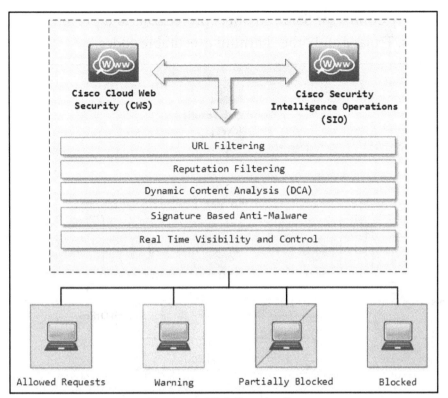

Figure 1-2: Web Security flow

Cisco Cloud Web Security Server or ScanSafe Proxy Servers are deployed all over the world, entertaining the user by securing and defending their web traffic. It inspects the elements of each and every web page of a website. Every element is inspected such as if a web page element includes HTTP, Flash, and Java. All of these elements will be inspected. This inspection is depending upon the policies configured at the Cisco Cloud Web Security Portal. In result, Web page is allowed, partially blocked or Blocked. These policies are necessary to prevent Over Blocking and Under Blocking as well.

Cloud Web Security Connectors for IOS

Cisco Cloud Web Security CWS offers IOS and ASA Connectors. These CWS Connectors are used for extending or integrating the security features related to Cloud web security on IOS routers and ASA Firewalls. Cloud Web Security Connector can be used for firewall features, VPN, Intrusion Prevention features. This connector is along with Security K9 License of Cisco. These CWS Connectors helps in advanced web security and strong protection against Website. These Cloud Web Security connectors can be deploying over Integrated Services Router (ISR) to route the Web traffic to the Web Security Cloud to monitor, filter and inspect in detailed and enforce security policies over web traffic. By using Integrated Services Routers ISR, network can be deployed between Wide area, such as Head office and Branch office, Site to Site connection of a corporate network etc. Cisco

Cloud Web Security Connector Solution offers protections and prevention against worms, viruses, backdoors, Trojans and other harmful executable codes.

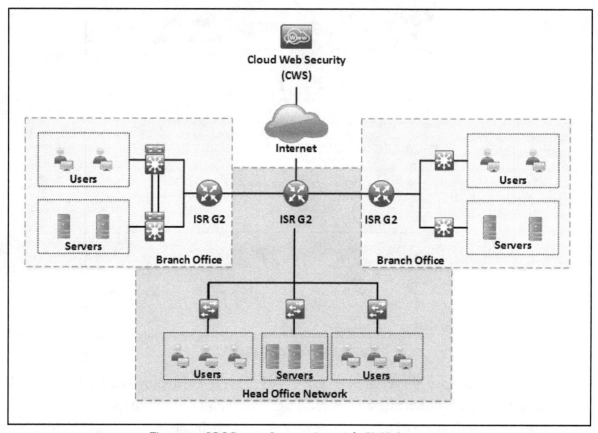

Figure 1-3: IOS Router Integration with CWS Connector

IOS Cloud Web Security Connector Configuration

Configuring CWS Proxy Servers
ISR(config)# parameter-map type cws
//Configures a Global CWS parameter MAP
ISR(config-profile)# server primary ipv4 {IP Address} port http 8080 https 8080
//Configures Primary Server for HTTP and HTTPS traffic
ISR(config-profile)# server secondary ipv4 {IP Address} port http 8080 https 8080
//Configures Secondary Server for HTTP and HTTPS traffic
ISR(config-profile)# license 7 {License Key}
//Configures CWS License

Configuring Source interface to Proxy Server
ISR(config-profile)# source interface {Interface name}
//Configuring Source Interface for Redirection
ISR(config-profile)# timeout server 5
//Server keep alive time
ISR(config-profile)# timeout session-inactivity 3600

```
//Session inactivity time in Seconds
```
ISR(config-profile)# user-group marketing username superuser
```
//Configuring default usergroup
```
ISR(config-profile)# server on-failure block-all
```
//Block all traffic when CWS Server can not communicate with Web Server
```
ISR(config-profile)# user-group exclude {Groupname}
```
//Exclude group
```
ISR(config-profile)# user-group include {Groupname}
```
//Include Group
```

Configuring Scanning Interface

ISR(config)# interface {Interface name}
```
//Configure CWS traffic scanning interface
```
ISR(config-if)# cws out
```
//Content scanning for Egress traffic
```
ISR(config-if)# ip virtual-assembly in
```
//Configuring VFR on ingress
```
ISR(config-if)# ip virtual-assembly out
```
//Configuring VFR on egress
```
ISR(config-if)# end

Troubleshooting Commands for IOS

ISR# Show content-scan history
```
//Displays content scanning History information.
```
ISR# Show content-scan statistics
```
//Session Slow information
```
ISR# Show content-scan
```
//Displays content scanning information.
```
ISR# Show cws history
```
//Displays content scanning history
```
ISR# Show cws
```
//Displays content scanning information.
```
ISR# Show ip admission cache
```
//View User status
```
ISR# Show content-scan statistics memory-usage
```
//CWS Entries, connections, and Web Request
```
ISR# Show content-scan statistics failures
```
//Shows Number of failure
```
ISR# Show content-scan session active
```
//Show individual Active sessions
```

Cloud Web Security Connectors for ASA

Using Cisco ASA Firewall integrated with Cisco Cloud Web Security Connector, offers enhanced and advanced Web Security and Control over the corporate network. Network along with Network Devices and datacentres can be secured through deployment of Firewalls integrated with CWS Connectors without any additional physical hardware deployment with great performance and throughput. Web Security features can be deployed more effectively with respect to User-enrolled on External Datastore such as Active Directories as well as Mobility and Remote access can also be supported using Cisco AnyConnect Secure Mobility Client Application. Cisco CWS Connector for ASA offers protection of Clients from Web threats regardless of Location and devices, Monitoring and Controlling of Web traffic without compromising over security, Reducing Cost and Complexity in term of deployment of Additional Hardware. Using ASA CWS Connectors, all Web traffic is automatically redirected to Cisco Cloud Web Security Data Centre for inspection.

Hardware Requirement for CWS Connector

Cisco ASA 5500 and 5500-X Series with version 9.x or later can be integrated with Cisco Cloud Web Security.

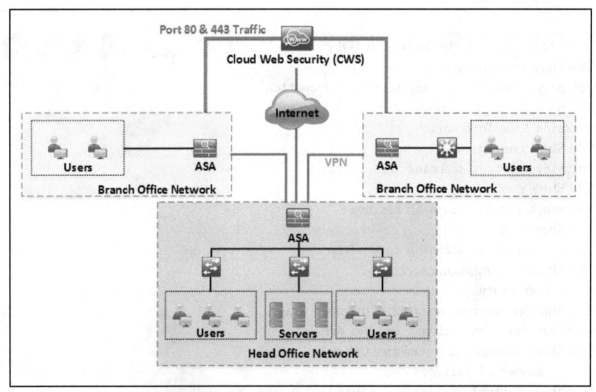

Figure 1-4: ASA Firewall Integration with CWS Connector

Cisco Cloud Web Security (CWS) works on ASA in Routed mode only. It redirects the Web traffic (HTTP and HTTPS) to the Cloud Web Security Servers. These Web Security Proxy Servers on Cloud filters, inspect and scan the redirected web traffic and compare against configured policies in CWS or Cisco ScanCenter. The redirected Web traffic will be permitted, warned or blocked according to the policies. ASA can also be deployed with Identity firewall to Authenticate and Authorized the users with respect to AAA rules. Policies are configured as per User to authenticate and Authorized them as well as User based reporting.

Figure 1-5: CWS or ScanCenter Portal Page

Authentication Key

There are two types of authentication keys offered by Cisco Cloud Web Security or ScanCenter. This Authentication key is required to authenticate the company associated with the Web traffic by Cloud Web Security.

1. **Company Authentication key**

These keys are to enable the Cloud Web Security feature on multiple ASAs. Administrator have to generate the key in ScanCenter and it will be emailed for use. Administrator can generate this key by accessing the URL:

https://scancenter.scansafe.com/portal/admin/login.jsp

2. **Group Authentication Key**

Group Authentication key is a unique key per ASA. Group Authentication key enables Web Security feature on ASA and identify the redirected web traffic associated with the ASA.

Whitelists:

Whitelists are the lists configured on the device to permit the traffic according to configured Policies and Rule as Blacklists blocks the traffic. Whitelists in ASA for Web Traffic Security required AAA or IDFW configuration to bypass the Cloud Web Security redirection. Web traffic from specific authenticated users or group of users are authorized to bypass the redirection of web traffic to the Cloud Web Security Servers for inspection. The Web request directly route to the web servers without redirection through Proxy Servers as other user's web requests do. This Whitelist feature can be configured as per user or per group instead to IP address. Whitelist configuration is not necessary but configured optionally according to the requirement.

CWS does not support ASA Clustering, SSL Clientless VPN, and does not support ASA CX module. Cloud Web Security feature only support IPv4 addressing only.

Class Map Traffic	Cloud Web Security Inspection
From IPv4 to IPv4	Supported
From IPv6 to IPv4 (using NAT64)	Supported
From IPv4 to IPv6	Not Supported
From IPv6 to IPv6	Not Supported

Table 1-1: CWS IP Scheme Support

ASA Cloud Web Security Connector Configuration

Configure Access Lists

Access-list are configured for redirecting Web traffic i.e. HTTP and HTTPS. Recommended is to configure two ACLs for each HTTP and HTTPS traffic which will help in monitoring and inspection of packets processing through CWS.
 	
ASA(config)# access-list web extended permit tcp any any eq www
`// Access Control List for HTTP traffic`
ASA(config)# access-list https extended permit tcp any any eq https
`// Access Control List for HTTPS traffic`

Configure Class Maps

Configure the Class maps for Web Traffics and associate the Access Control List to them.
ASA(config)# class-map cmap-http
ASA(config-cmap)# match access-list web
`// Class Map for HTTP traffic`
ASA(config)# class-map cmap-https
ASA(config-cmap)# match access-list https
`// Class Map for HTTPS traffic`

Configure Inspection Policy Maps

ASA(config)# policy-map type inspect scansafe http-pmap
ASA(config-pmap)# parameters
ASA(config-pmap-p)# default group httptraffic
ASA(config-pmap-p)# http
`// Inspection for HTTP Traffic`
ASA(config)# policy-map type inspect scansafe https-pmap
ASA(config-pmap)# parameters
ASA(config-pmap-p)# default group httpstraffic
ASA(config-pmap-p)# https
`// Inspection for HTTPS Traffic`

Configure Policy Maps

ASA(config)# policy-map pmap-webtraffic

ASA(config-pmap)# class cmap-http

ASA(config-pmap-c)# inspect scansafe http-pmap fail-close

```
// Policy Map for HTTP traffic
```

ASA(config-pmap)# class cmap-https

ASA(config-pmap-c)# inspect scansafe https-pmap fail-close

```
// Policy Map for HTTPS traffic
```

Configure Service Policy

ASA(config)# service-policy pmap-webtraffic interface inside

Configure Cloud Web Security on the ASA

ASA(config)# scansafe general-options

ASA(cfg-scansafe)# server primary ip {IP Address} web 8080

ASA(cfg-scansafe)# retry-count 5

ASA(cfg-scansafe)# license {Licence Number}

```
// Configuring CWS Connector
```

Troubleshooting Commands for ASA

ASA# show user-identity user active list detail

```
//Show the Active users
```

ASA# Show user-identity ad-agen

```
//Showing AD Agents information
```

ASA# Show service-policy inspect scansafe

```
//Showing number of connections redirected or whitelisted
```

ASA# Show scansafe server

```
//Show reachability of Cloud Web Security Proxy Servers
```

Cisco AnyConnect Web Security Module

Cisco AnyConnect Secure Mobility Client's Web Security Module is an application that is deployed on the endpoint device to forward the web traffic towards Cisco Cloud Web Security proxy server or ScanSafe server to inspection. AnyConnect Configuration and functionality is controlled by AnyConnect Web Security Client Profile editor. Cisco AnyConnect Web Security Module deployment requires.

Requirement	Version
ASA	v8.4(1)
ASDM	v6.4(0)104
Operating System	Windows XP SP3 x86 (32-bit)
	Windows Vista x86 (32-bit) or x64 (64-bit)
	Windows 7 x86 (32-bit) or x64 (64-bit)
	Mac OS X v10.6 x86 (32-bit) or x64 (64-bit)
	Mac OS X v10.7 x86 (32-bit) or x64 (64-bit)
	Mac OS X v10.8 x64 (64-bit)

Table 1-02: Cisco AnyConnect Web Security Module Requirement

Cisco AnyConnect Web Security Module offers two types of deployment of Web Security License.

1. **Web Security Deployed as a Standalone Component**

   This standalone license deployment doesn't need to install VPN or requirement of ASA. Deployment requires AnyConnect License as well as Cisco Cloud Web Security License.

2. **Web Security Deployed as a Component of AnyConnect**

   AnyConnect Web Security Module will work with AnyConnect Essentials or Premium without AnyConnect License for Web Security However Cisco Cloud Web Security license will be required.

Cisco AnyConnect Secure Mobile Client Web Security module Deployment

1. Download Cisco AnyConnect Secure Mobile Client ISO image
2. Extract ISO image file of Cisco AnyConnect Secure Mobility Client
3. Customize the Web Security Module by installing Standalone Profile Editor
4. Download and Install AnyConnect Profile Editor.

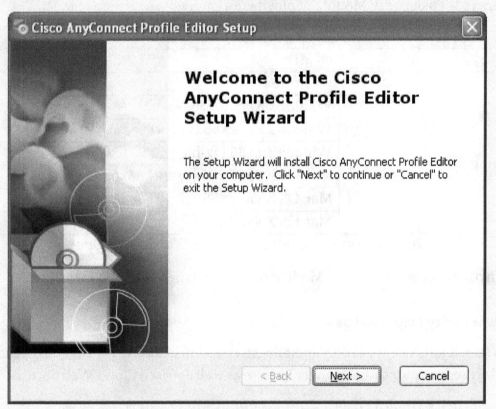

Figure 1-6: Cisco AnyConnect Profile Editor Installation Wizard

5. Run AnyConnect Profile Editor & create Any Connect Web Security Client Profile.
6. Create Web Security Profile (Add Web Security Profile file in extracted ISO file location)
7. Install Customized Web Security Module

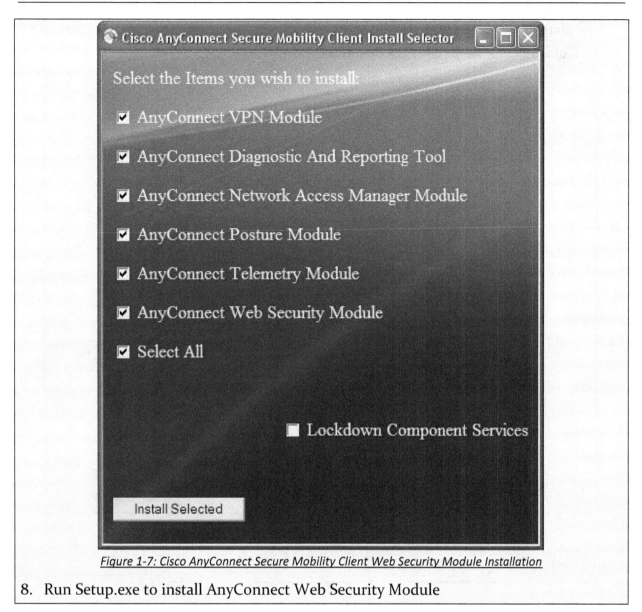

Figure 1-7: Cisco AnyConnect Secure Mobility Client Web Security Module Installation

8. Run Setup.exe to install AnyConnect Web Security Module

Web Usage Control

Web Usage Control offers Dynamic Content Analyzes to provide enhanced security in efficient manner. Cisco Web Usage Control feature is available in S-Series Cisco Web Security Appliance which ensures the advanced, next level security solution for URL Categorization. It monitors, analyze, and block the objectionable content over 50 percent ratio.

Dynamic Content Analysis Engine

Dynamic Content Analysis Engine controls are web access request by categorizing the URL dynamically. These categorization is done by inspecting the web traffic received as a response of web request from the web server. It is not possible to take action and block the content when request is just sent or before receiving of response. Once URL is inspected

and validated by Dynamic Content Analysis engine, it stores it into temporary cache which provide quick response for the next requests.

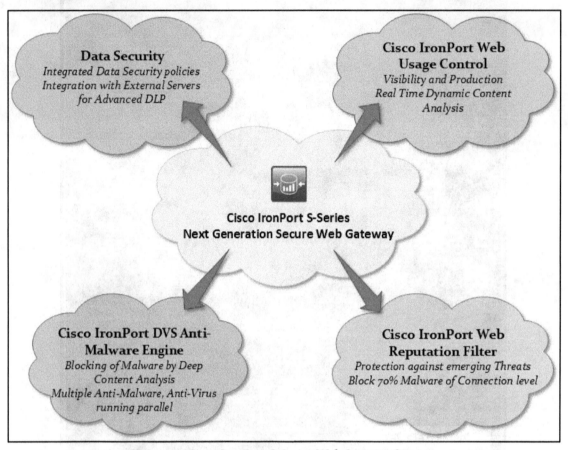

Figure 1-8: Cisco IronPort S-Series Web Security Gateway

Mind Map

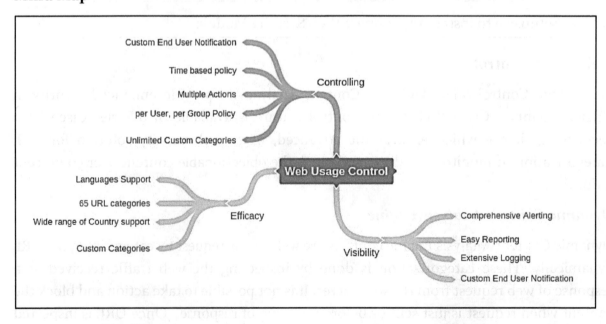

Cisco Web Security Appliance (WSA)

Introduction

Securing a corporate network from rapidly increasing internet world day by day is not possible using a single solution. Advance threats and attacks are always a risk to the vulnerability of the Network and resources. Protection and defense against these advanced Web Security threats requires a Web Security solution which should be strong enough to secure against multiple, advanced, and severe attacks from Endpoint to Edge Router. Increasing demand of Secure Remote connectivity and Mobility is also a great challenge for IT World to deploy the Security Solution fulfilling all requirements. Cisco offers Web Security Appliance (WSA) which is combined integrated solution of Strong Defense and Web protection, Visibility and Controlling Solutions.

Cisco Web Security Appliance (WSA) is integrated Solution of the following Security Solution

1. Advanced Malware Protection (AMP)
2. Cognitive Threat Analytics (CTA)
3. Application Visibility and Control (AVC)
4. Policies
5. Reporting
6. Secure Mobility

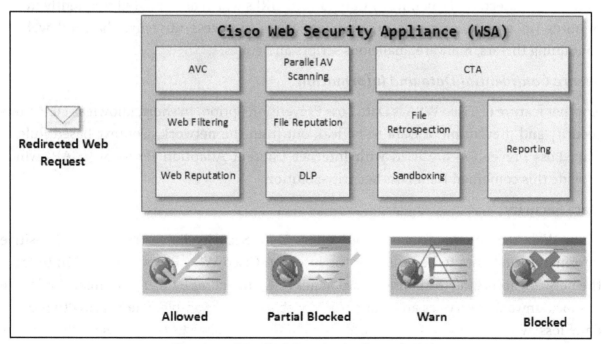

Figure 1-9: Cisco Web Security Appliance (WSA)

Features and Function of Cisco Web Security Appliance

Advance and Strong Protection against Malwares

Cisco Web Security Appliance in combination of Cisco Cloud Web Security (CWS), Cisco Advanced Malware Protection (AMP), Cisco Cognitive Threat Analytics (CTA) offers Next level advance protection against Web Security threats. This all-in-one High Level Web Security gateway provide the array of Web Security deployment features.

Integration with Cisco Identity Service Engine (ISE)

Cisco WSA can also integrate with Cisco ISE for efficient, flexible, scalable and responsive enhanced Web security.

Visibility and Control

Hundreds of Application including a wide range of Micro application visibility and Controlling can be enforced using policies through Web Security Appliance. Using this visibility and controlling feature, an application can partially be allowed. An example is a running application of Social Web Site with some blocked features like Chat, File Upload or Download by WSA.

Usage Control

Dynamically update of URL in URL Database and Dynamic Content Analysis offers real time Web Protection. Dynamically Categorized URLs which are updated frequently in few minutes (in every 3 to 5 minutes) prevent users to access unsecure, harmful website containing threats, malware, malicious scripts and codes.

Secure Confidential Data and information

Another feature of Cisco WSA is Data Loss Prevention option. In short, known as DLP offers security and prevention of Data to be leak out from the network, Context-based Rule in Data Loss Prevention are used with Internet Content Adaption Protocol (ICAP) which provide this combined Data Loss Security Solution.

Data Security

Cisco Web Security Appliance (WSA) offers Data Security by restricting the Sensitive information and data to be sent over the internet. Cisco WSA Block information to leave the network according the configured policies to ensure compliance. Administrator is able to block unwanted services and feature on a web site. For example, File Sharing to prevent data loss while allowing other features of the web page. Context based rules offers protection of sensitive and confidential information from sending out the network. These Context-based Rule can be implemented using Data Loss Prevention (DLP) or Integrated with DLP and Internet Content Adaptation Protocol (ICAP).

Cisco Data Security Filtering can be enabled on Cisco Web Security Appliance. If Data Security is enabled over WSA, it ensures the evaluation and scanning of the Web traffic that is leaving the network. Data Security Policies offers the configuration of policies which are used by the scanning and evaluation process to filter and block the specific type of upload requests. Data Security Policy evaluated the outbound data traffic for evaluation of its compliance with respect to the associated data security policy. Cisco Web Security Appliance (WSA) scan the data traffic for Data Security otherwise external scanning servers can also be integrated via configuring External Data Loss Prevention Policies.

Data Security feature offered by Cisco Web Security Appliance (WSA) manage the scanning and filtering of the data traffic uploading over web. The protocol request that are supported and monitored by Cisco Data Security feature are Hyper Text Transfer Protocol (HTTP), Decrypted Secure-HTTP (HTTPS) and File Transfer Protocol (FTP).

Configuring Data Security Policy

1. Navigate to the *Web Security Manager > Cisco IronPort Data Security page or the Web Security Manager > External Data Loss Prevention page.*

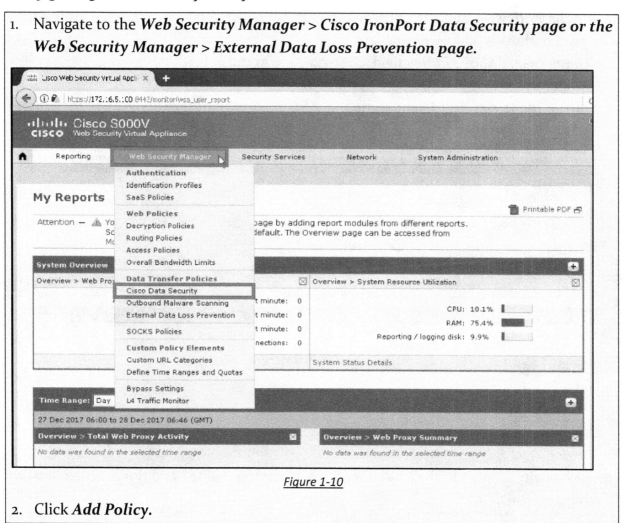

Figure 1-10

2. Click *Add Policy.*

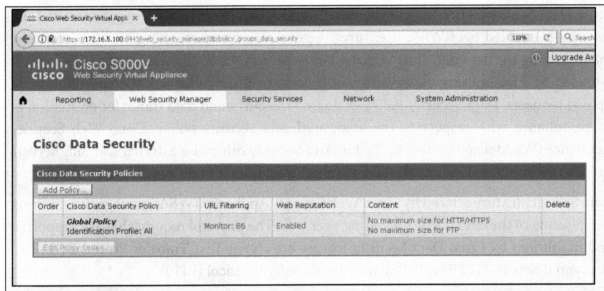

Figure 1-11

3. In the **Policy Name** field, enter a name for the policy group, and in the **Description** field, optionally add a description.

4. In the **Insert Above Policy** field, choose where in the policies table to place the policy group.

5. In the **Identities and Users** section, choose one or more Identity groups to apply to this policy group.

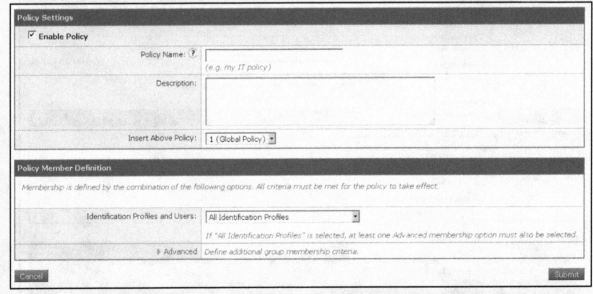

Figure 1-12

6. Optionally, expand the **Advanced** section to define additional membership requirements.

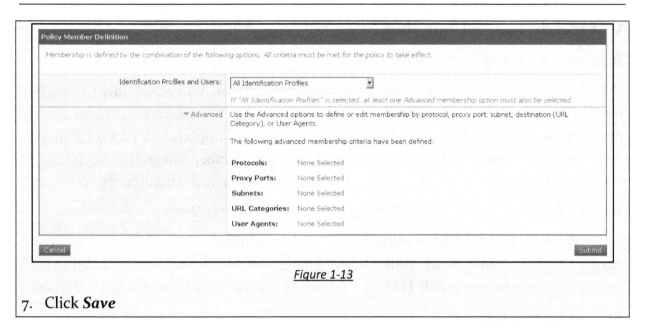

Figure 1-13

7. Click **Save**

Mind Map

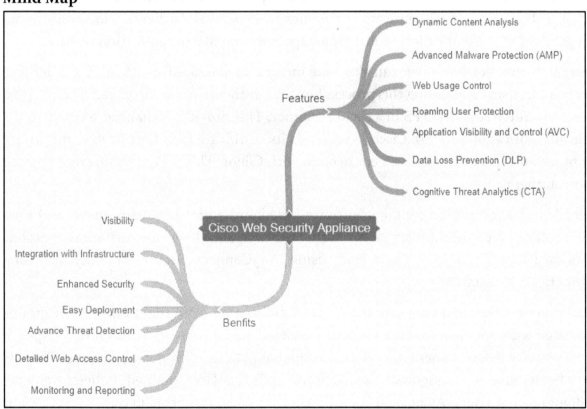

WSA Identity and Authentication

Integration with Active Directory (AD)

Cisco Web Security Appliance (WSA) offers the support of the Active Directory (AD) server for End User credentials. Kerberos, NTLMSSP and Basic Authentication scheme can be deployed using Active Directory. Kerberos scheme is not supported in Cloud Connector mode; it is only supported in standard mode. Active Directory integration supports the HTTP, HTTPS, FTP over HTTP, Native FTP, and SOCKS (Basic Authentication) protocol.

Integration with Lightweight Directory Access Protocol (LDAP)

Cisco Web Security Appliance (WSA) also offers the support of Lightweight Directory Access Protocol (LDAP). Basic Authentication scheme can be deployed using LDAP. LDAP integration supports the HTTP, HTTPS, FTP over HTTP, Native FTP, and SOCKS protocols.

Authentication Process

Credentials or Attributes or the Authentication realm are configured over Active Directory or LDAP which are later asked to be compared against configured Authentication policy. Authentication realms are the details which are required to contact authentication servers and also the details of authentication schemes used. Global Authentication settings are independent of authentication protocol and applied over all Authentication realms.

External Authentication server can also have integrated like LDAP or RADIUS. Credentials which are transmitting during this process between authentication server can be encrypted to be transmitted over HTTPS in a secure manner. This provides enhanced security to the basic authentication process. Cisco WSA sends its certificate (Self Certificate) and private key by default to a secure HTTPS connection with Client. This secure connection ensures secure authentication.

User Identification profile contains Software-based authentication requirement and User Identification methods information. Authentication and User identification methods includes using Cisco ISE, Cisco ASA using AnyConnect Secure Mobility or using Authentication realm.

Policies are configured to manage the Web traffic coming from the users or User groups associated with the Identification profiles. These policies are classified into several types in Cisco WSA by default. These are predefined global policies with default actions. There is also the feature to configured User defined policies. User defined Policies requires configuration of Users, Associated Identification profiles, Protocols like HTTP HTTPS or FTP to communicate with the devices, Proxy ports to access web proxy, Subnets, Time ranges, Predefined or custom URL categories, User Agents or Application.

Transparent User Identification

In the ordinary User identification process, users are identified and authenticated when the user provides the login credentials which may be the Username and Password to the prompting login form. These credentials are validated by the authentication server and then that user is authorized and enforcement policies are applied associated with that specific user or user group.

The Transparent User identification feature offered by Web Security appliance (WSA) ensures the identification and authentication of a user without prompting to provide login credentials at the endpoint user. Transparent User identification requires a trusted source to be deployed to provide these credentials on behalf of the End user.

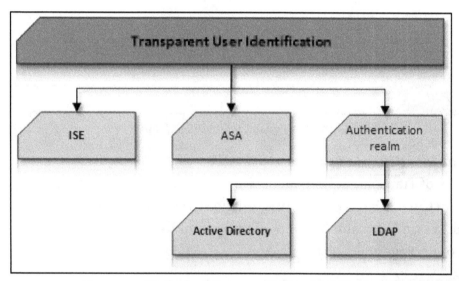

Figure 1-14: Methods of Transparent User Identification

There are the three methods for the Transparent Authentication of Users.
1. Transparent Identification of users with ISE
2. Transparent Identification of users with ASA
3. Transparent Identification of users with Authentication realms
    a. Active Directory
    b. LDAP

Transparent Identification of users with ISE

Transparent user identification with ISE requires the Cisco ISE with pxGrid and ISE Admin Certificates. These certificates can be generated or uploaded over Cisco ISE and these certificates are exported to Cisco WSA for identification. ISE server must be properly integrated with WSA by enabling Auto Registration, ISE server footer section configured with pxGrid Service in Connected state to pxGrid, Configuring of Security Group tags and policies associated with these SGT's.

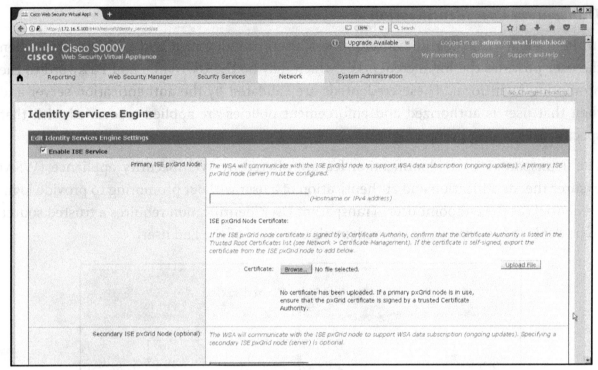

Figure 1-15: ISE Configuration Option

Transparent Identification of users with ASA

In the process of Transparent User identification with Cisco ASA, identification is done by Mapping from Cisco Adaptive Security Appliance (ASA). This Mapping received from Cisco ASA is IP address to Username mapping. Transparent user identification with ASA requires Cisco AnyConnect agent enabled with ASA.

Cisco AnyConnect Secure Mobility Client is the Endpoint agent which is required for transparent End user identification. This Endpoint agent is responsible for sending the endpoint information such as User IP address and username to the Web Security Appliance (WSA) through integration with ASA. Using Cisco AnyConnect client, Remote user (Connected through VPN) and local User configuration can be implemented.

Transparent Identification of users with AD

Transparent User Identification using Active Directory can be deployed using Windows Network, NT LAN Manager (NTLM) or Kerberos. Transparent User identification is to be enabled and a Separate Active Directory agent is required such as Cisco Context Directory Agent (CDA). CDA is responsible for query the Active Directory Security logs to extract the information about users that are authenticated because Active Directory does not record users log in logs in a manner that can be easily extracted by the other devices such as Web Security Appliance (WSA). Multiple Active Directory can be deployed to provide high availability. Active Directory transparent user identification cannot integrate with LDAP authentication; it functions with Kerberos or NTLM independent of LDAP.

Transparent Identification of users with LDAP

Web Security Appliance deployment with integration of LDAP uses IP address to username mapping for authentication. When user logs in, its attributes are compared by the eDirectory client configured as LDAP. Upon successful authentication, users attribute such as IP address is recorded in LDAP. Deployment of Transparent user identification using LDAP requires eDirectory Client installed on every client device which is used to authenticate the client from LDAP. LDAP server is responsible for updating the Network address (IP address) of the client and record it.

Web Usage Control

Rapidly increasing Internet with billions of new Website addition day by day also increase the risk of violation of compliance. It costs millions and billions of dollar to an organization in terms of Web threats decreasing the productivity and attack of their resources. Using Categorized List of static URL is not an effective approach to secure in every network architecture.

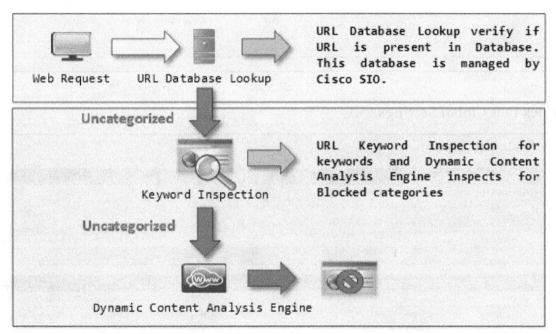

Figure 1-16: Cisco Web Usage Control

Cisco IronPort Web Security Appliance offers Web Usage Control which offers protection and Visibility and control not only List of URL Filtering as well as Real Time Dynamic listing. In Combination of Cisco Security Intelligence Operation (SIO) and Cisco IronPort Web Usage Control dynamically inspect the content using Content Analysing Engines which filters the Web Content into categories. This Globally deployed Cisco IronPort Web Security Appliance classify harmful and blocked content as dark web.

Configuring Dynamic Content Analysis and URL Filtering

1. Navigate to the **Security Services > Acceptable Use Controls** page.

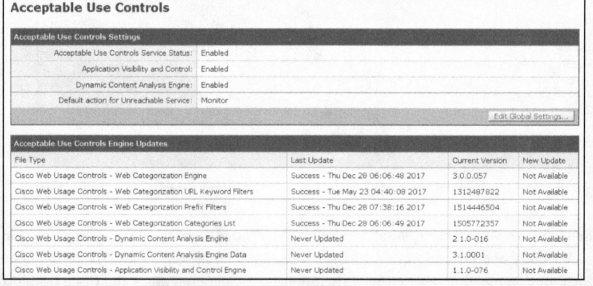

Figure 1-16

2. Click Edit **Global Settings.**

Figure 1-17

3. Verify the **Enable Acceptable Use Controls property** is enabled.

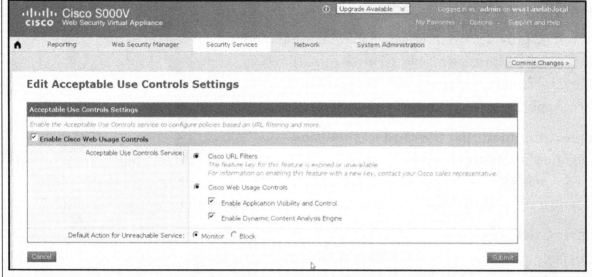

Figure 1-18

4. Choose whether or not to enable the **Dynamic Content Analysis Engine**.
5. Choose the default action the Web Proxy should use when the URL filtering engine is unavailable, either Monitor or Block. Default is Monitor.
6. **Submit** and commit your changes.

Application Visibility and Control (AVC)

Cisco Application Visibility and Control or AVC feature offers integrated solution at Application Layer. Cisco AVC offers State-full Deep Packet Inspection (DPI). This integrated Service Management Solution with Cisco ASR 1000 (Aggregation Service Router) performs State-full deep packet inspection at layer 7 of every application. Cisco AVC can handle and Control thousands of various types of Applications like Voice, Video, mailing, gaming and others. AVC can integrate with Cisco IOS/IOS XE device as well as external tools.

Application Visibility and Control (AVC) ensures controlled access over Web. Website offering features and service can be allowed with enhanced and more controlled manner. Using Application Visibility and Control AVC engine, websites such as Social Media Website which are more popular nowadays can be allowed in a controlled manner by blocking desired services for granular control.

Cisco AVC Monitors

Cisco AVC provides two methods for configuring monitors:
1. Performance Monitor(Full-featured)
2. Easy Performance Monitor (ezPM)

Cisco Application Visibility and Control offers the Following Features.

Application Identification and Recognition

Integrated Solution of Cisco AVC along with Cisco IOS, NBAR2 (Next-Generation Network Based Application Recognition) or IOS XE offers Deep Packet Inspect (DPI) which can recognize and identify thousands of applications from Network Layer to Application Layer.

Metric Calculation

With Network Monitoring Tools such as Netflow Metric Calculation and Collection is also managed & reported like Bandwidth, response time, jitter, latency & packet loss.

Reporting

Deep Packet Inspection (DPI) is used for Management and Reporting the resources, metrics, application and network performance and helps in troubleshooting as well.

Recommended IOS Platforms

Platform	License
Cisco ISR G2 (880 series)	Appx License
Cisco ISR G2 (890 series)	Appx License
Cisco ISR G2 (1900, 2900, 3900 series)	Appx License

Table 1-03: Recommended IOS Platform for AVC

Recommended IOS XE Platforms

Platform	License
Cisco ASR 1001-5G, ASR 1001-X, and ASR 1002-X	AVC License
Cisco CSR1000V (Premium)	AVC License
Cisco ISR 4000 Series	Appx License

Table 1-04: Recommended IOS XE Platform for AVC

Enabling AVC Engine

1. Navigate to the **Security Services > Acceptable Use Controls** page.

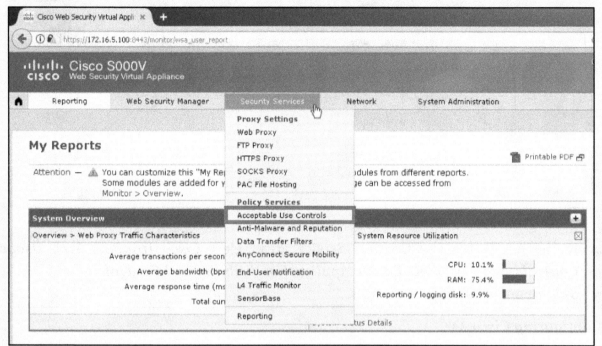

Figure 1-19

2. Click Edit **Global Settings.**

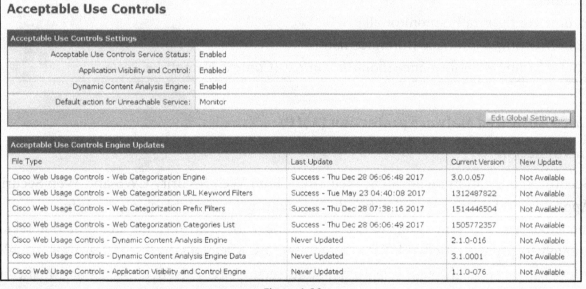

Figure 1-20

3. Verify the **Enable Acceptable Use Controls property** is enabled.

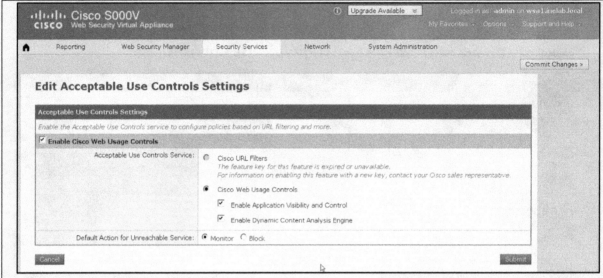

Figure 1-21

4. In the Acceptable Use Controls Service area, select **Cisco IronPort Web Usage Controls**, and then select **Enable Application Visibility and Control.**

5. **Submit** and commit your changes.

Configuring Cisco AVC

Router(config)# Performance monitor context {Context Name} profile {Profile Name}

Router(config)# exporter destination {IP Address} source {Source Interface} port {port number}

Router(config)#traffic-monitor all

Router(config)# Interface {Interface name}

Router(config)# Performance monitor context {Context Name}

Cisco Advanced Malware protection (AMP)

Introduction

Secure Web Solution deployment including Cloud Web Security CWS and Web Security Appliance WSA secure the network by identifiying and blocking harmful websites, malicious content and categorizing URL along with URL filtering are still not secure enough to protect a network from vulnerabilities. Malicious traffic and viruses can also affect the network through a legitimate and secure site. Advance threats and malicious traffic requires a more powerful and advanced security system to protect the network which cannot be done by using basic threat detection, Application Controlling, URL filtering and Security Policies.

These advanced Malwares and Vulnerability of downloading viruses from secure sites need an advanced web security solution which protect the network by monitoring the traffic and analysis, inspect and filter the malicious traffic continuously. Cisco offers Advanced Malware protection (AMP) for protection of Web with Cognitive Threat Analysis (CTA) for more enhanced security and performance to be integrate with Web Security Appliance for a complete Web Security Solution.

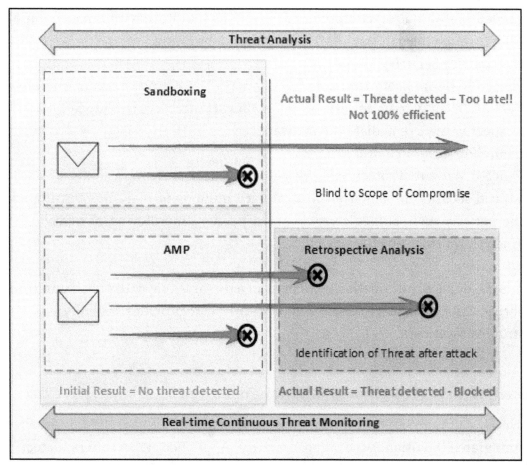

Figure 1-22: Retrospective Analysis with Cisco AMP

Features and Advantages of Advance Malware Protection

1. Advanced Threat Recognition

Advanced Malware Protection AMP ensures enhanced threat detection & comprehensive security by protecting against web threats & malwares. AMP's security services provide protection before attacks, during the attack in process & after.

2. Real time Continuous Protection

Advanced Malware Protection offers Continuous monitoring and inspection of traffic passing through the gateway. AMP monitors, analyze, and keep records.

3. Retrospective Security

Advanced Malware Protection not only offers real time protection but also ensures the protection even when an attack or malicious activity is detected later; AMPs Retrospective alert remediate the malware.

4. Extreme Performance and Efficiency

Advanced Malware Protection is designed to deal with high loads of data traffic. Advanced security intelligence can deal with millions of malwares passing with data traffic per day such as files correlation, inspection, monitoring of behaviour against advanced, and emerging threats.

5. Sandboxing

This is the detailed information of analysis of a threat, along with behaviour, threat level of threat detected while accessing your network. It provides visibility and complete control over Network.

Advanced Malware Protection (AMP) with Cognitive Threat Analysis (CTA)

Cognitive Threat Analysis is a complementary solution with Advanced Malware Protection AMP. Integrated Solution with Web Security Appliance WSA offers detection and remediation from advanced, sophisticated threats. Integrated Web Security Solution offers

- Automatic Identification, Observation of malicious and suspicious web data.
- Monitoring & validation of logs, alert and information by the web security devices.
- Identification of anomalous activities based on normal behaviour.
- Device behaviour identification

Configuring Web Reputation and Anti-Malware in Access Policies

1. Navigate to the **Web Security Manager > Access Policies page**.

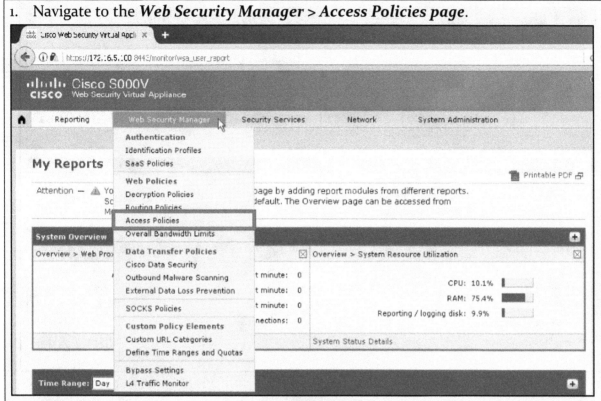

Figure 1-23

2. Click the **Web Reputation and Anti-Malware Filtering** link for the Access Policy you want to configure.

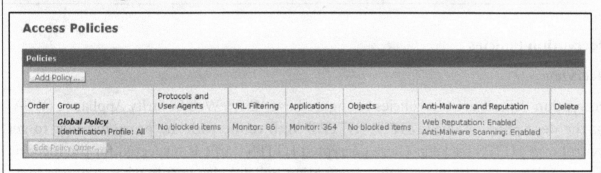

Figure 1-24

3. Under the "**Web Reputation and Anti-Malware Settings**" section, choose **Define Web Reputation and Anti-Malware Custom Settings** if it is not chosen already.

4. In the **Web Reputation Settings** section, choose whether or not to enable **Web Reputation Filtering**. Adaptive Scanning chooses the most appropriate web reputation score thresholds for each web request.

Access Policies: Anti-Malware and Reputation Settings: Global Policy

Web Reputation Settings

Web Reputation Filters will automatically block transactions with a low Web Reputation score. For transactions with a higher Web Reputation score, scanning will be performed using the services selected by Adaptive Scanning.

If Web Reputation Filtering is disabled in this policy, transactions will not be automatically blocked based on low Web Reputation Score. Blocking of sites that contain malware or other high-risk content is controlled by the settings below.

☑ Enable Web Reputation Filtering

Advanced Malware Protection Settings

Advanced Malware Protection is currently disabled globally.

Cisco DVS Anti-Malware Settings

Feature Key for McAfee has expired or is unavailable.
For information on enabling this feature with a new key, contact your Cisco sales representative.

McAfee is currently disabled globally.

☑ Enable Suspect User Agent Scanning ☑ Enable Anti-Malware Scanning (Webroot, Sophos)

Malware Categories	Monitor ⊖ Select all	Block ⊗ Select all
⊖ Adware	✓	
⊖ Browser Helper Object	✓	
⊖ Commercial System Monitor	✓	
⊖ Dialer	✓	

Figure 1-25

5. Scroll down to the ***Cisco IronPort DVS Anti-Malware Settings*** section.
6. Configure the anti-malware settings for the policy as necessary.
7. ***Submit*** and commit your changes.

Decryption Policies

Overview

Decryption Policies are the Policies configured over Cisco Web Security Appliance (WSA) for the decryption of Secure-HTTP (HTTPS) Web traffic with the proxy in order to get control over HTTPS packets. These decrypted HTTPS traffic is inspected for the meeting the compliance condition and rules. Decryption policies also ensure what action is to be taken to the requests which do not meet the compliance criteria containing invalid or revoked security certificates. Decryption policies handle the HTTPS traffic by ensuring when HTTPS traffic is to be decrypted.

Decryption Policies Deployment Scenario

Decryption Policies can be configured in the Web Security Solution deployment where requirements may be:
- Inspection of Encrypted Traffic
- Decryption of HTTPS traffic and enforcement of Content-based Access Policies.
- Scanning of Malware in HTTPS traffic
- Monitoring of Request leading to Drop. Pass through or Decrypt action.
- Dropping of HTTPS connection.

Configuring Decryption Policy Actions

Actions	Description
Monitor	Monitor option in Decryption policy to ensure the inspection or scanning of the generating requests against the conditions and control settings which leads to take decision of final action to be enforced over the generated request.
Drop	Drop option simply drops the connection. Cisco Web Security Appliance WSA will drop down the HTTPS Web connection requests passing through, user will not be notified that the web security devices have dropped the connection request.
Pass through	If Web Security Appliance is configured with Pass through Option, the generating web connection request will pass and proceed to the destination server without any inspection and evaluation of the content in the requesting packet. Standard Pass-through option however ensures the inspection validity check of request using HTTPS handshaking with the server to validate the Server certificate validity. If server fails, communication will be blocked.
Decrypt	Decryption option offers the decryption of HTTPS traffic. Using Decryption option encrypted traffic generating with in the network can be decrypted, scanned for malwares, checked against condition and policies. Decrypt option is used for application of Access policies over decrypted HTTPS traffic and scanning of malwares.

Table 1-05: Decryption Policy Actions

Controlling HTTPS Traffic

Decryption policies configured over We Security Appliance for HTTPS connection request, Control settings are associated with these decryption policies for the controlling of HTTPS traffic. These control settings ensure the application whether to decrypt, pass through or drop the connection request.

Option	Description
URL category	Pre-defined or custom URL categories can be inspected for the application of configured action to be taken over HTTPS request. User defined (custom) URL category can be configured for pass through or drop for permitting or denying particular web connection request, similarly for pre-defined URL categories. Decryption option can also be applied over URL categories for application of Access Policies.
Web Reputation	Decryption Policy action can be configured for HTTPS requests according to the web reputation. Web reputation of the requested server is inspected to take the configured action over these request
Default Action	Default action can be configured to take action if none of the any control settings applied. **Default Action:** Apply when no decision is made by URL categories and Web Reputation. **Web Reputation disabled:** If Web reputation is disabled, it will apply Monitor action on URL Category. **Web Reputation enabled:** if Web reputation is enabled, it will apply Monitor action on website having no score.

Table 1-06: Control Setting Options

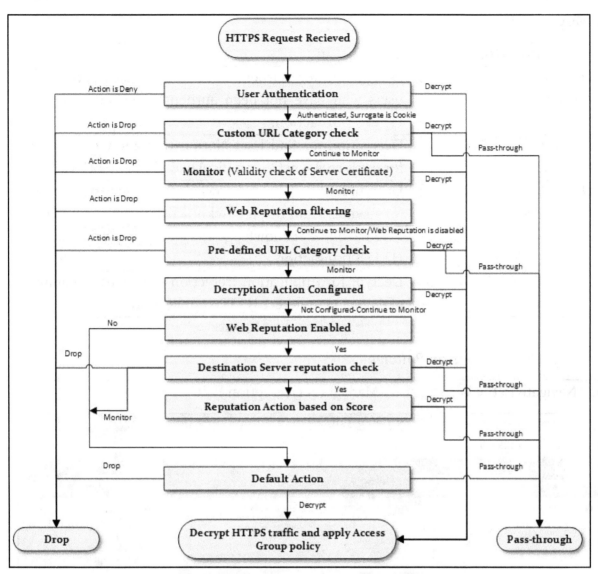

Figure 1-26: Decryption Policy Operation Flow

Decryption Options

Decryption Option	Description
Decrypt for Authentication	Decryption for authentication allows decryption for users who have not been authenticated, prior to this HTTPS transaction.
Decrypt for End User Notification	Decryption for End User Notification allow decryption for users so AsyncOS can display End User Notification.
Decrypt for End User Acknowledgment	Decrypt for End User Acknowledgment allow decryption for AsyncOS can display Acknowledgment of End User who have not acknowledge the web proxy prior to this HTTPS transaction
Decrypt for Application Detection	Decrypt for Application Detection Enhances the ability of AsyncOS to detect HTTPS applications

Table 1-07: Decryption Options

Configuring Decryption Policies

1. Navigate to the Web Security Manager > Decryption Policies page.

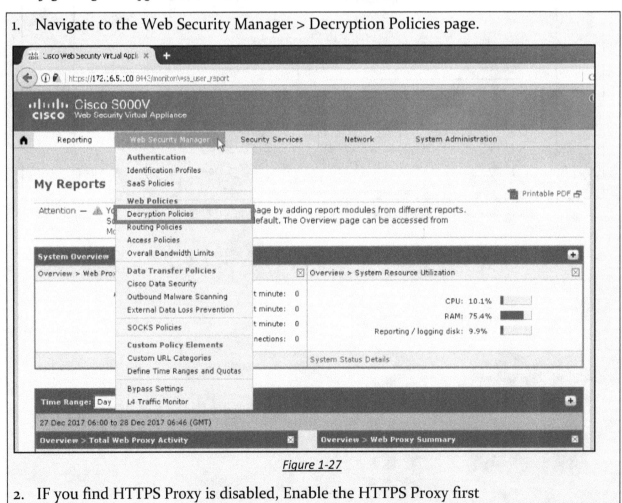

Figure 1-27

2. IF you find HTTPS Proxy is disabled, Enable the HTTPS Proxy first

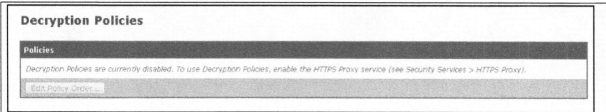

Figure 1-28

3. Go to *Security Services > HTTPS Proxy* and Enable HTTPS Proxy. Click *Enable and Edit Settings*

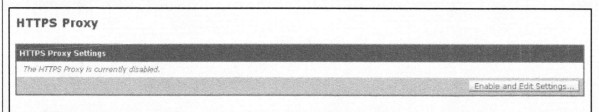

Figure 1-29

4. Edit Certificate Settings & Submit to enable HTTPS Proxy

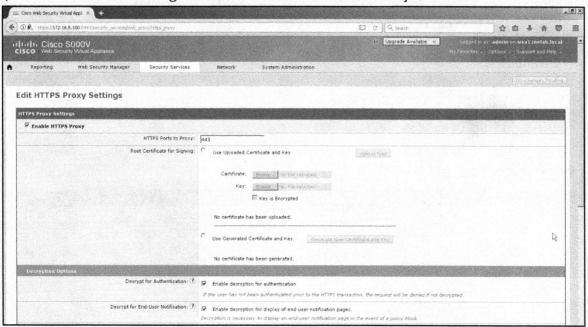

Figure 1-30

5. Click Add Policy.

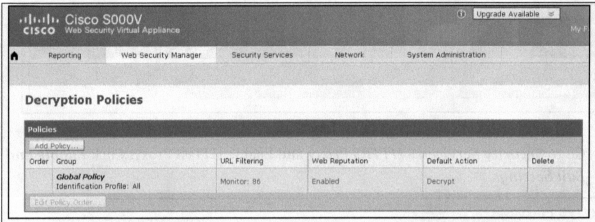

Figure 1-31

6. In the Policy Name field, enter a name for the policy group, and in the Description field, optionally add a description.

7. In the Insert Above Policy field, choose where in the policies table to place the policy group.

8. In the Identities and Users section, choose one or more Identity groups to apply to this policy group.

9. Optionally, expand the Advanced section to define additional membership requirements.

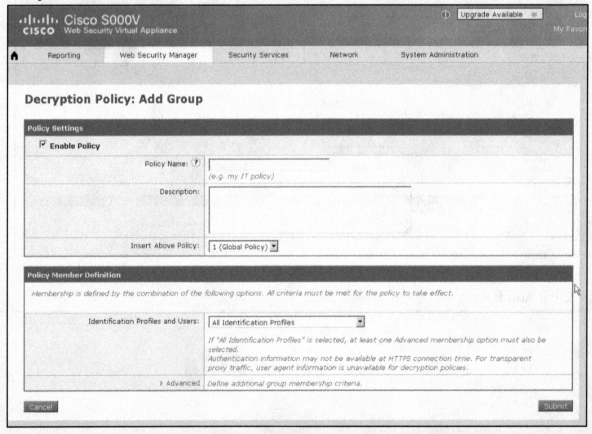

Figure 1-32

10. To define policy group membership by any of the advanced options, click the link for the advanced option and configure the option on the page that appears.

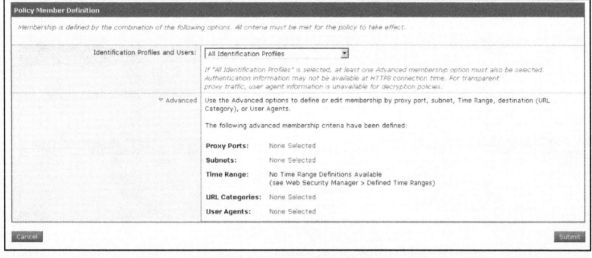

Figure 1-33

11. Submit your changes

Traffic Redirection & Capture Methods (Explicit Proxy vs Transparent Proxy)

Installation of Web Security Appliance (WSA) requires planning of how traffic will be redirected to WSA. Cisco Web Security Appliance WSA is not deployed in the network in inline, it becomes the most challenging step of integration of WSA in web security deployment to lie in between user and requested web servers for scanning the requests. There are two possible solutions to redirect the web traffic to WSA.

- Explicit Proxy Deployment
- Transparent Proxy Deployment

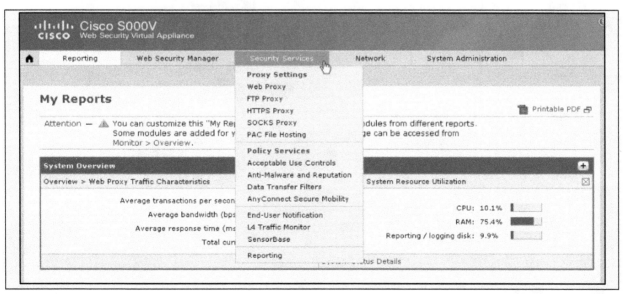

Figure 1-34

Go to *Security Services* tab, and Click *Proxy Settings*

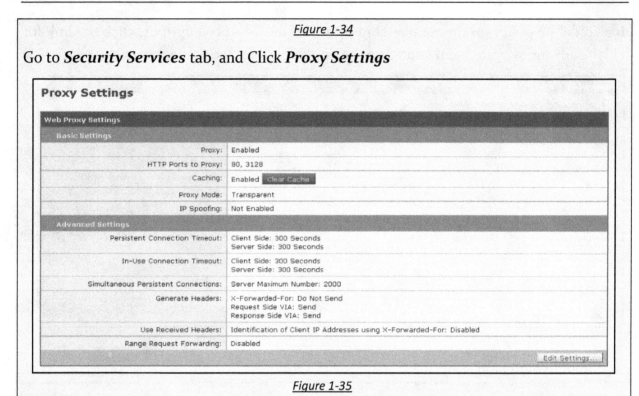

Figure 1-35

Click *Edit Settings*

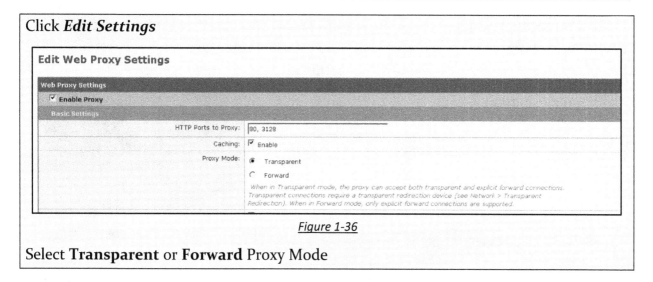

Figure 1-36

Select **Transparent** or **Forward** Proxy Mode

Explicit Proxy

Explicit Proxy Deployment option is the combined solution with firewall which blocks the traffic which is not generating from WSA. In this deployment of Explicit proxy, Client Proxy Application with configuration to use proxy like WSA has to be configured. Administrator will have to configure the Proxy setting to every client, it is simple and easy to deploy as proxy aware applications are known with the proxy settings.

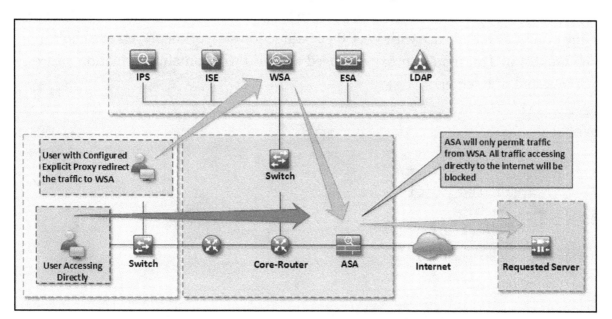

Figure 1-37: Traffic Redirection using Explicit Proxy

Explicit proxy deployment can also be used to test WSA and other Web Security Solution deployment components as it does not depend upon anything else. Web request in Explicit proxy deployed scenario will contain destination address of the Proxy server.

Transparent Proxy

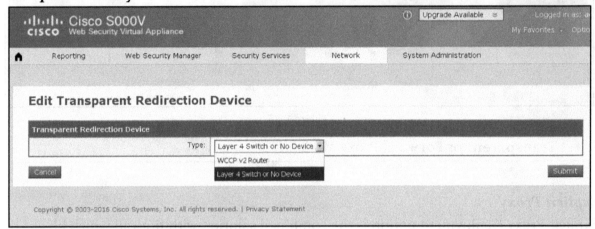

Figure 1-38: Transparent Proxy

Another method of redirecting the Web traffic to the Web Security Appliance WSA is by using Transparent Proxy Deployment. Transparent Proxy can be deployed over the network point where all data traffic using Port 80 (possibly port 443) can be redirected to the WSA through a network device. Network Device can be a Cisco Adaptive Security Appliance ASA or any other network device with WCCP v2 redirection support deployed at a choke point. Web request in Transparent proxy deployed scenario will contain destination address of the requested web server.

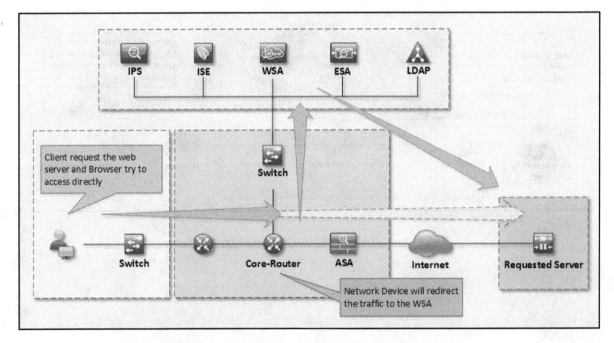

Figure 1-39: Traffic Redirection using Transparent Proxy

Traffic Redirection Options and their Configuration Methods

Deployment	Method	Description
Transparent Proxy	Layer 4 Switch (PBR)	A Layer 4 switch is used to redirect based on destination port 80
	WCCP	A WCCP v2 enabled device (typically a router, switch, PIX, or ASA) redirects port 80
	Bridging Mode	Dual NICs, virtually paired. Traffic goes in one NIC and out the other (not available)
Explicit Proxy	Browser Configured	Client browser is explicitly configured to use a proxy
	.PAC fie Configured	Client browser is explicitly configured to us a .PAC file, which in turn, references the proxy

Table 1-08: Redirection Deployment Option and Methods

Cisco Email Security Appliance

Technology Overview

Email Spamming

Email Spam which is also known as Junk Email, is the unsolicited number of Emails. Email users normally face this problem of receiving spam emails. These spam emails may be based on advertising of something as well as containing malware and malicious objects that can be downloaded if the user clicks the object in these spam emails.

Email Spamming are of different types. Spamming is typically used for frauds, promoting inexpensive things like pharmaceutical drugs, shopping, jobs and others. Free rewards and offers of discount coupons get the attention of email receivers. A spam sender does this through a fake process and story asking the victims for payments.

Another Spam Email are phishing emails, which are disguised as official organizations email. For example, a Spam email disguised as the email from a bank may lead the receiver to submit its login credentials by clicking the fake (but exactly the same as official web page is). Users should avoid these spam email and don't click on any link in the spam emails.

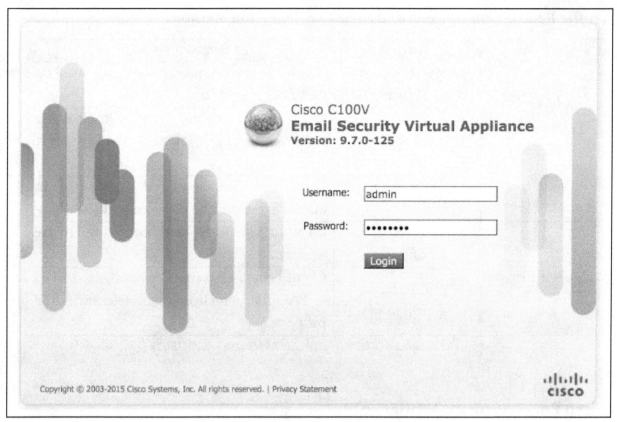

Figure 1-40: Cisco Email Security Appliance Portal Page

Spam-Filter Solution

An Email security solution will become useless and non-effective if spam & unsolicited emails—is not filtered properly. In every corporate network of organizations, requirement of Email is necessary. It is required to filter irrelevant emails from the email traffic including legitimate emails which belong to the corporate network. Spam Filter is a software program that is used to detect spam email and prevent unwanted email. Certain threshold or criteria is needed to be set for filtering Email. Using Anti-spam solution to inspect and filter these spam email not provide complete solution from preventing spam. False positive and incorrect detection of emails can block legitimate mail and can also allow spam. Reducing the threshold of filtering will user responsible to identify spam email manually. Use of Anti-spam solution is not as reliable as to rely only over it.

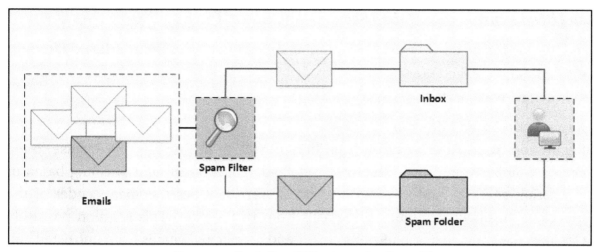

Figure 1-41: Basic Email Filtering using Spam Filter

Cisco IronPort Email Security Appliance

Cisco IronPort Email Security Appliance (ESA) provide protection of Emails and Employees using Email infrastructure. Cisco ESA can be easily integrated into deployed network with high flexibility. Email security Appliance can be deployed as single interface filtering Emails of internal Mail server. Another deployment method includes two interfaces, one for Emails from internet and another from internal Servers.

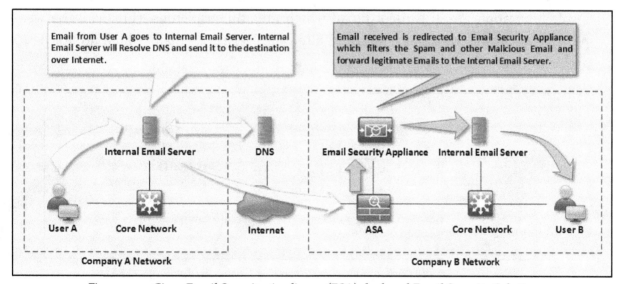

Figure 1-42: Cisco Email Security Appliance (ESA) deployed Email Security Solution

Spam Filtering using Cisco Email Security Appliance (ESA)

Spam Filtering can be done by using Reputation based filtering or Context based filtering.

- Reputation based Filtering
- Context based Filtering

1. Reputation based Filtering

Reputation based Filtering offers front line protection or first layer of defense to the network. Reputation based filtering can defend against spam and phishing based of reputation checking and inspection. If the server identifies the spam sender of the malicious emails, it will block the emails from that sender. This solution positively classifies the spam emails, malicious emails and unsolicited emails from untrusted and potentially harmful hosts. Inspection of malwares and malicious activity in email is inspected using Anti-Virus scanning.

Reputation filtering compare the reputation data from Cisco SenderBase. Cisco SenderBase global repository for Email Security which records reputation of Hosts. When any Host is involved in Malicious or Potentially harmful activities, it lowers the reputation of that host. Comparing the information from Cisco SenderBase, by Reputation filtering supported device such as Cisco Email Security Appliance ESA legitimate Emails are proceeded to the next level of inspection and filtering. Email with lower reputation are discarded. Email which are still suspicious, (Emails in between positive email which passes reputation filter and Negative Emails which do not pass), are inspected before delivering.

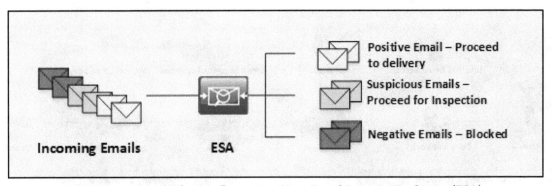

Figure 1-43: Email Filtering flow using Cisco Email Security Appliance (ESA)

2. Context based Filtering

Context Based Filtering is also offered by Cisco Email Security Appliance. In Context based filtering, complete content of the email including images, attachments and other details like embedded URL are inspected. This is the next level of defense which provide next level inspection to the reputation filter.

Feature & Functions

Global Threat intelligence

Integrated solution offer Global threat intelligence, ensures High performance and strong Email protection powered by Cisco Talos. Visibility provides real time foot print view over traffic. hundreds of terabytes of Security intelligence information are handled daily. Talos updates in every 3 to 5 minutes updating millions of security devices connected through it.

Spam Filtering

As defined, Cisco Email Security Appliance offers spam filtering using multi-layer filtering techniques using Reputation based filtering and Context based filtering provide front layer protection. Contextual inspection, Auto classification and other filters and integration with Anti-virus and AMP offers enhanced Spam filtering.

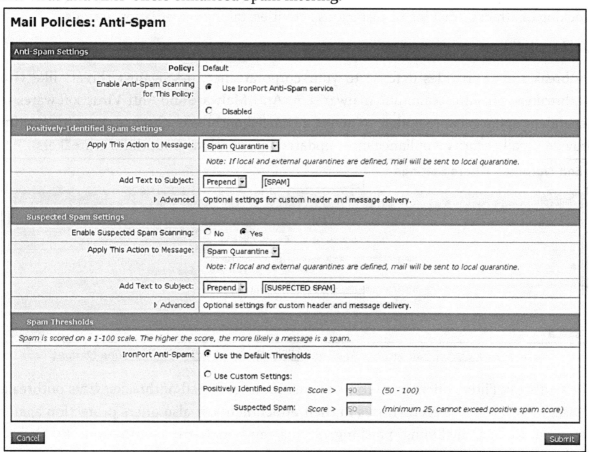

Figure 1-44: Cisco Email Security Appliance (ESA) Spam Filtering

Graymail Detection

Graymail detection feature offers detection of graymails such as marketing emails, advertising emails, and other number of emails. Graymail offers Monitoring, Classification of these emails along with unsubscribe option. Graymail detection and un subscription protects from Malware from unsubscribed link and offer management of Subscription with visibility.

Advanced Malware Protection

Cisco Email Security Appliance ESA also includes Cisco AMPs. Using AMPs feature, Sandboxing, Retrospection and continuous inspection can be done before and after processed from Email gateway. Reputation scoring and blocking strengthen the reputation based filtering. Advanced Malware protection also offers increased performance of blocking of attacks, tracking of suspicious activities, taking remediation actions.

Outbreak Filters

Outbreak filters provides defense to your corporate network against threats like virus Outbreakers, phishing scams and malwares. As Anti-Malware and Anti-Virus soft wares are dependent upon software update to detect advanced outbreaks, Cisco updates in real-time provide Email Security Appliance most updated information about the Outbreakers.

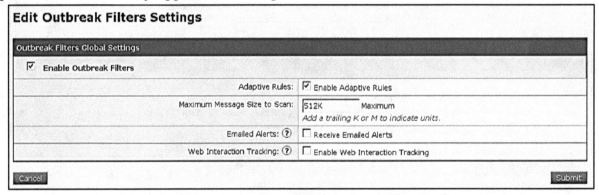

Figure 1-45: Cisco Email Security Appliance (ESA) Outbreak Filter Configuration Options

The Outbreak Filters offers protection against message-based outbreaks; virus outbreaks, Messages never-before-seen viruses in their attachments. it also offers protection against non-viral threats, including phishing, scams, and malware distribution. By default, Outbreak Filters scans incoming and outgoing messages for possible threats.

Tracking

Web tracking requires full integration of Email Security Solution deployment which ensures to track the Users including user of clicked Malicious or Potentially Harmful URLs, Top level Malicious URLs that are accessed by End Users including Date, Time, Reason of

rewritten and remediation action on certain URL. This tracking is offered by report from ESA.

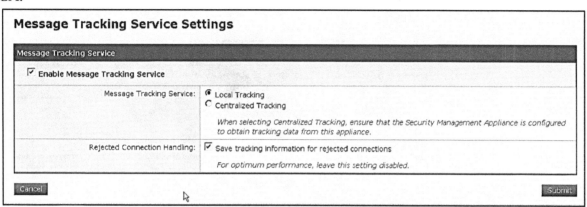

Figure 1-46: Cisco Email Security Appliance (ESA) Message Tracking

Data Loss Prevention

Configuring Data Loss Prevention polices keep your personal, secret, and confidential information secured. It ensures that this information will not leave the network based on the pre-configured policies or user defined custom polices. Cisco Email Security DLP engine configured with DLP policies make few false positives. The DLP engine monitor classify violations by severity, offering application of different levels of remediation action. Remediation action can also have configured to be taken in cases of violation.

Flexibility

Cisco Email Security Solution offers ease of deployment that can be adjusted with every network architecture. Using System Setup wizard, even complex network can be controlled easily. Support of Virtual and Hardware deployment in a same deployment scenario offers same level of security for local and remote locations of your corporate network.

Cisco Email Encryption

Cisco Email Encryption feature offers security in terms of encrypting the email traffic. Encryption of email is associated with the configured encryption profile containing information regarding characteristics of encryption and key server identification information. There are two types of key server which may either be Cisco Registered Envelope Service (CRES) or Cisco Encryption Appliance.

Email Encryption Work Flow

In a network scenario with Email Encryption, Cisco Email Security Appliance or Cisco Email Encryption Appliance encrypts the content of the email. Encryption algorithm used by these encryption devices are ARC (Alleged Rivest Cipher 4) or AES (Advanced Encryption Algorithm). ARC4 also known as RC4 is common and preferred choice normally

because it can provide strong encryption and minimum decryption delay for the receiving user, whereas AES also provide Strong encryption but it takes time to decrypt causing delay for recipient.

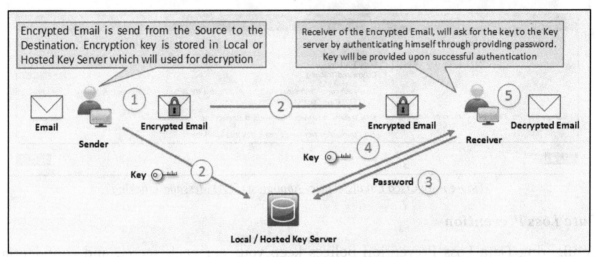

Figure 1-47: Email Encryption work flow

Encryption key will be forwarded to be stored in Local Key server or Hosted Key server. When receiver gets the Encrypted email, recipient is authenticated through its password (Password assigned at the time of register of encryption service as authentication credential to be authenticated by the Key server) and the decrypted message will be shown.

Key Servers

- **Cisco Registered Envelope Service (CRES)**
  Cisco Registered Envelope Service (CRES) secure the email traffic via sending encrypted message through registered envelopes. Registered Envelopes are those encrypted emails which may be password protected. Password is required for the authentication of every user. If a new user is connected in the email encryption environment, it has to register with the service to set password. This password will authenticate him.

- **Cisco Email Encryption Appliance**
  Cisco Email Encryption Appliance like IronPort Encryption Appliance offers email encryption solution which secure the email traffic regardless of Public Key infrastructure or any other agent of receiving side. Cisco IronPort Email Encryption Appliance ensures the encryption for secure communication, satisfy the compliances required by the corporate network. It provides ease of use on any platform with universal accessibility.

Integrated Functions

Cisco Email Encryption can also be used with the integration along with Cisco Email Security Appliance for the high performance and enhanced security including services:

- RSA Email Data Loss Prevention (DLP)
- Cisco IronPort Anti-Spam
- Cisco IronPort Outbreak Filters

Enabling Email Encryption on Cisco Email Security Appliance

1. Click Security Services > Cisco IronPort Email Encryption.

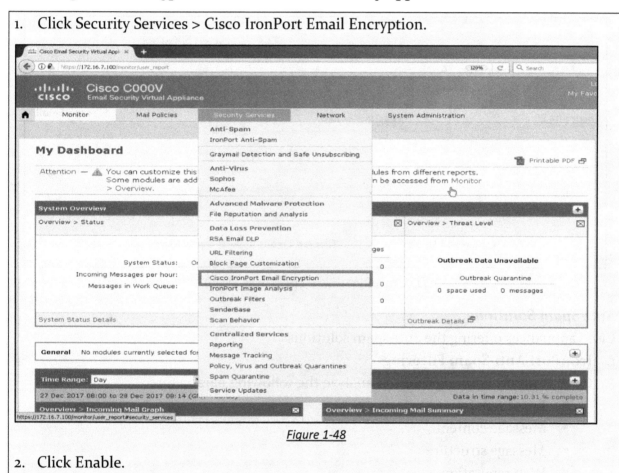

Figure 1-48

2. Click Enable.
3. Click Edit Settings to configure the following options (optional):
    A- Configure maximum message size to encrypt, Cisco's recommended size is 10 MB. The maximum encryption limit is 25 MB.
    B- Email address of the encryption account administrator.
    C- Configure a proxy server.

Anti-Spam Policies

Anti-Spam Technology Overview

Anti-spam is the process of scanning and filtering the email traffic including incoming and outgoing mails based on the associated Anti-spam policies configured on the Email Security Appliance. One or more than one filtering devices can be integrated to scan the traffic. Scores are assigned to every message which help to analyze, differentiate and finally filter the traffic with respect to the categories including Not Spam, Suspected Spam and Positively Identified as Spam.

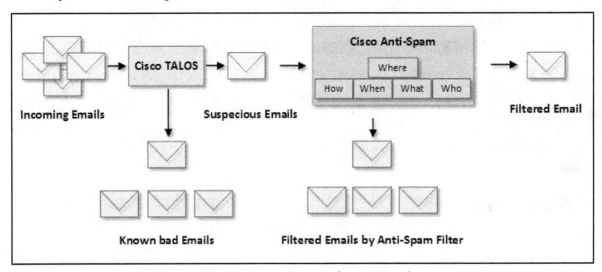

Figure 1-48: Anti-Spam Defense in Depth

Anti-Spam Solutions

Cisco appliances offering the anti-spam solutions:

1. **IronPort Anti-Spam Filtering**

   Cisco IronPort Filtering solution analyze the following parameters

   - Email reputation
   - Message content
   - Message structure
   - Web reputation

2. **Cisco Intelligent Multi-Scan Filtering**

   - Initially, Email is scanned through third party Anti-spam scanning engines.
   - Cisco Intelligent Multi-Scan forward the results and reports of these Third Party Anti-Spam Scanning Engines to the Cisco Anti-Spam which finally decide the verdict.
   - After Cisco Anti-Spam scanning, forward combined multi-scan score to AsyncOS.
   - Combined, compared result of Multi-Scanning offers low False Positive results.

Key Steps to configure Anti-Spam Scanning on Email Security Appliance

- Enable Anti-Spam Scanning on Email Security Appliance. Email Security Appliance has 30 days' evaluation feature key for Cisco IronPort Anti-Spam Filtering, and Cisco Intelligent Multi-Scan also required feature key to offer its services. To enable one or both of these solutions, Feature key will be required.
- Configure the spam email filtering, to quarantine spam emails into local Email Security Appliance or in External Security Management Appliance.
- Define the Group to be inspected for Spam.
- Recommended option is to enable SenderBase Reputation Service.
- If Cisco ESA is not connected directly to the recipient, make sure that incoming massage include original Sender's IP address if it is coming through relay, such as Mail Transfer Agent or Mail Exchange.
- Prevent alert messages by ESA from being incorrectly identified as spam.
- Enable URL filtering to strengthen protection.

Configuring the Default Anti-Spam Policies for Incoming Messages

1. Navigate to *Mail Policies > Incoming Mail Policies*

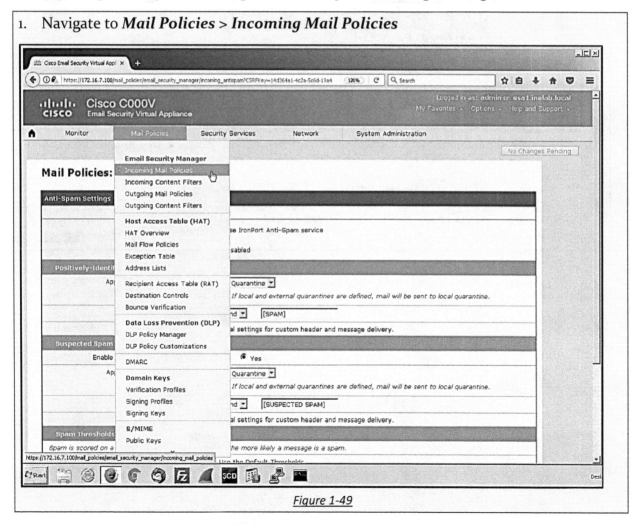

Figure 1-49

2. Click the link for the *anti-spam security service*.
3. In the "*Positively Identified Spam Settings*" section, change the "*Action to apply to this message*" to Drop.

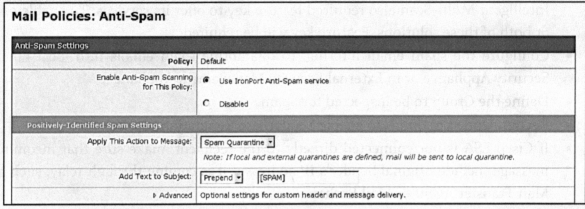

Figure 1-50

4. In the "*Marketing Email Settings*" section or *Suspected Spam Setting*, click *Yes* to enable marketing email scanning.

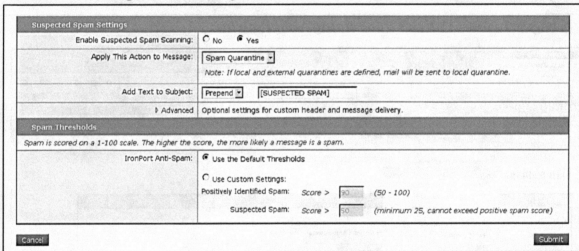

Figure 1-51

5. Click *Submit*.

Virus Outbreak Filter

Outbreak Filters

Outbreak filters offers protections of the network from small and large scale virus attacks including viral and non-viral attacks, phishing and other malicious attacks. Most of Anti-virus and Anti-malware software application also protects against these malicious and potentially harmful attacks to the network but they are unable to detect latest, advanced outbreaks unless a software update in available on internet and updated on systems and devices. Cisco continuously collect the information and remediation action which are updated on Email Security Appliance in real time which protects the network from latest malwares.

Cisco uses traffic pattern to create rule which are helpful and criteria to classify the packet incoming the network as safe or outbreak. Incoming traffic may not completely an outbreak, but it can also be the part of the outbreak. These packets are separated from the safe traffic for further inspection unless are determined to be safe and delivered or harmful and blocked. Updates regarding new outbreaks are updated by McAfee and Sophos.

Features of Outbreak Filter

- **Delay**
  Outbreak filter separates the message from the incoming traffic that are part of Outbreaks or suspicious to be the part of outbreaks. Outbreaks may include Virus Outbreaks or Non-Viral Outbreaks. When these packets are separated, Security appliance is updated regarding the latest updated information. It will then rescan for validating the packet to be the part of outbreak.

- **Redirect**
  Outbreak filter redirect the recipient through proxy server if user is attempting these websites involved in non-viral attacks. proxy server redirection shows the warning regarding website containing malwares if website is operational. If the website is taken down, it shows an error message to the recipient.

- **Modification**
  Modification in terms of rewriting URL in non-viral threat messages indicating a warning for the user about the content of message by modification and adding a disclaimer.

Virus Outbreak Filter

Outbreak filtration offers the security against virus outbreaks which are message-based outbreaks and the non-viral outbreaks including threats, phishing, scam, malware etc. The default behaviour of Outbreak filter is scanning for virus outbreaks, Non-Viral threat filtering has to be enabled additionally if anti-spam scanning is enabled on the security

appliance. Feature key for any of the Anti-Spam filter is required, Anti-Spam or Intelligent Multi-Scan for running Outbreak filter scanning.

Virus Outbreak filters filter the messages based content which are never seen before. These viruses are the latest viruses which cannot be detected through anti-virus and anti-malware application as they are not continuously updated on real time. It also scans the attachment for never seen before threats. The most critical time is the window of time during which the virus is released till the anti-malware and virus vendors updates its information and definition. In this vulnerable time, these viruses can propagate globally taking the networks unsecure.

Cisco Security Intelligence Operations (SIO)

Cisco Security Intelligence Operation (SIO) offers the central security system which gathers the information regarding threats, information from Reputation services and other globally deployment security systems. This collection of information helps in sophisticated validation of malicious activities leading to enhanced secure protection and efficiently faster response time. Component on which Cisco SIO depends are

- SenderBase
- Threat Operation Centre
- Dynamic updates

Threat Level	Risk	Description
0	None	There is no risk that the message is a threat.
1	Low	The risk that the message is a threat is low.
2	Low/Medium	The risk that the message is a threat is low to medium. It is a "suspected" threat.
3	Medium	Either the message is part of a confirmed outbreak or there is a medium to large risk of its content being a threat.
4	High	Either the message is confirmed to be part of a large-scale outbreak or its content is very dangerous.
5	Extreme	The message's content is confirmed to part of an outbreak that is either extremely large scale or large scale and extremely dangerous.

Table1- 09: Cisco SIO Threat Level

Cisco Security Intelligence Operation SIO collect the real-time information from global SenderBase to the traffic patterns to classify the traffic and identify the anomalies leading to the outbreaks. Threat Operation Centre TOC compares and identify the outbreaks and set the certain threat level for the outbreaks. Cisco Email Security Appliance or other Web Security Appliance are dynamic updates with the information through Dynamic Update.

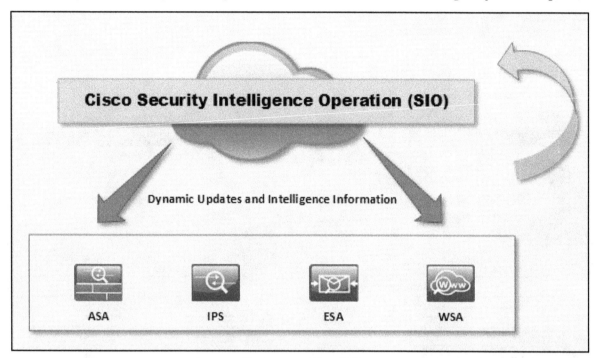

Figure 1-52: Cisco SIO

Configuring Outbreak Filters Global Settings

1. Click **Security Services > Outbreak Filters.**

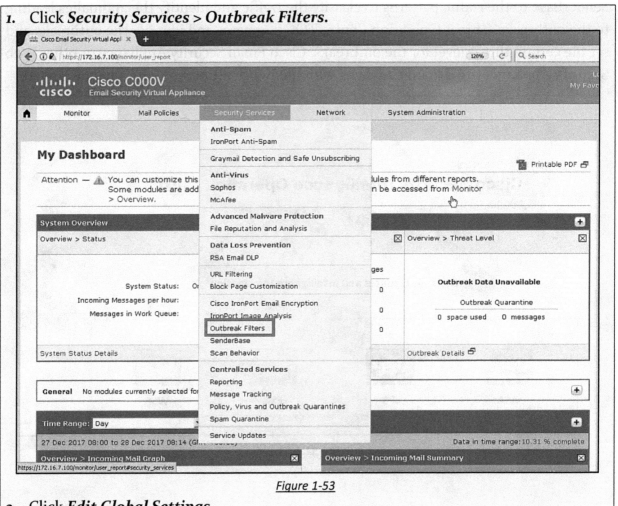

<u>Figure 1-53</u>

2. Click **Edit Global Settings.**

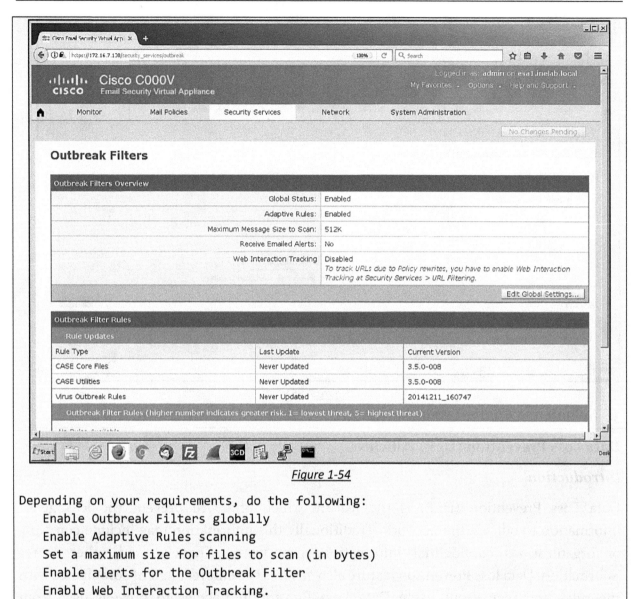

Figure 1-54

Depending on your requirements, do the following:

    Enable Outbreak Filters globally
    Enable Adaptive Rules scanning
    Set a maximum size for files to scan (in bytes)
    Enable alerts for the Outbreak Filter
    Enable Web Interaction Tracking.

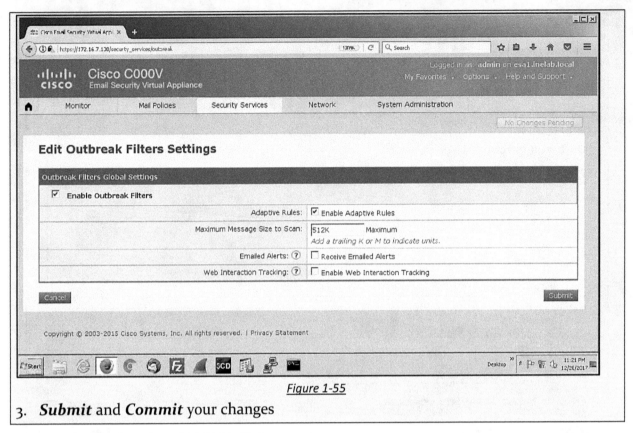

Figure 1-55

3. **Submit** and **Commit** your changes

Data Loss Prevention (DLP) Policies

Introduction

Data Loss Prevention (DLP) is the feature which offers to prevent the leakage of information to outside the network. Traditionally this information may include company or organizations confidential information, proprietary, financial and other secret information. Data loss Prevention feature also ensures the enforcement of compliance with the rules and regulations using Data Loss Prevention policies to prevent user from intentionally or unintentionally sending this confidential information.

Data Loss Prevention Scanning

- The User or Employee of an organization laying within the corporate network sends the Email to the recipient outside the network as Data Loss Prevention secure the information from leaving the network. Emails within the network are not scanned. Email Security Appliance ESA acting as the gateway for Emails incoming or outgoing the network.

- Email Security Appliance (ESA) completes its other processes such as inspection for Virus and malware or spam, till Data Loss Prevention Scanning, Email is in the Work Queue Stage.

- The Email Security Appliance scan the message content, header of the email, Attachments against containing sensitive data. This sensitive data is criteria is configured in Data loss prevention Policies.
- In case the Scanning process found sensitive information complying with the Data Loss Prevention Policy, Appliance protects the data by taking immediate action like Dropping the message, Quarantining, or delivering with restriction.
- In case the Security Appliance found nothing during scanning process, Email Security appliance delivers it to the recipient.

Data Loss Prevention Processes

When User or Employee from an organization sends an Email to a recipient which lies outside the organization, the Security appliance investigate for outgoing policy which applies to sender of the Email or recipient of that message, based on configured or pre-defined rules. The appliance inspects the body of the message using the Data Loss Prevention policies that are defined in outgoing mail policy.

The Email Security Appliance scan the content along with headers and attachments against the text, phrases, predefined patterns or expression that can be identified as sensitive content according to the associated Data Loss Prevention Policy.

The Email Security Appliance also scan and validate the context containing disallowed content to minimize false positive results. For example, content matching a Bank Account, credit card number or pattern as violation.

In the case the Email Security Appliance found matches more than one DLP policy, the first matching DLP policy will apply with respect to the configured order. Outgoing mail policy with multiple DLP policies configured over appliance, all policies use the result from a single content scan.

When Email Security Appliance detects potentially sensitive content during the scanning, the ESA assigns a risk factor between 0 - 100. This score indicates the that the Email contains a DLP violation.

Email Security Appliance then set the severity level as Critical or Low that is configured with respect to risk factor score, and performs the action specified for that severity level in the applicable DLP Policy.

Content Matching Classifiers in DLP Policy

Content matching Classifier in Data Loss Prevention policy offers the inspection and filtering against the expression, word, phrases configured in DLP Policy. These words may include anything traditionally Credit Card number, Bank Account numbers, Passwords and other information are used to restrict. For example:

123456789	(No match because of no supporting information)
Account : 123456789	(Match)
Account # 123456789	(Match)
Account number 123456789	(Match)

Configuring Content Matching Classifier

1. Select **Mail Policies > DLP Policy Customizations** and click **Add Custom Classifier**.

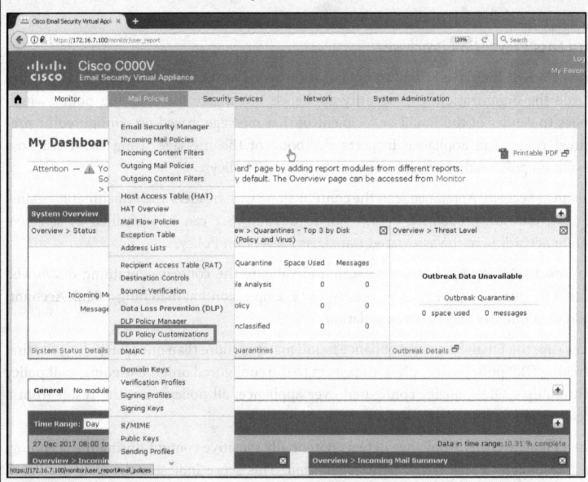

Figure 1-56

2. Enter a classifier name and description.
3. Enter a proximity and a minimum total score.
4. Choose one of the following detection rule types and define the associated content matching criteria:

     a-Words or phrases

     b-Text

     c-Regular expression

     d-Existing data loss prevention entity

5. Add additional rules by clicking Add Rule.

6. If you include multiple rules, specify whether All or Any rules must match.
7. Submit and commit your changes.

Message Filtering using DLP Policy

- **Message Filtering by Sender / Receiver**

Data Loss Prevention Policy can be configured precisely through filtering the message based upon the configured filtering option. DLP policy can be limit to filter the messages, which includes the recipients or senders or may not include the recipient or sender. Multiple entries can also be configured separated by comma or line break.

Option	Example
Full Email Address	user@ipspecialist.net
Partial Email Address	user@
All users in a domain	@ipspecialist.net
All users in a partial domain	@.ipspecialist.net

Table1- 10: Message Filtering options

- **Message Filtering by Attachment type**

Data Loss Prevention Policies can be configured to be precise through Filtering by attachment type. DLP Policy will limit scanning the messages that may or may not include the particular attachment type. Attachment category option offers the list of pre-defined attachment file type list. If the desired file type is not listed, you can also customize the file type. DLP policy can also be precise in scanning with respect to attachment size.

- **Message Filtering by Tag**

DLP Policy can also limit scanning for the message against a particular phrase. A custom message tag will be added when content filter found the compliance against DLP policy.

Creating DLP Policy Using Predefined Template

1. Select **Mail Policies** > **DLP Policy Manager.**

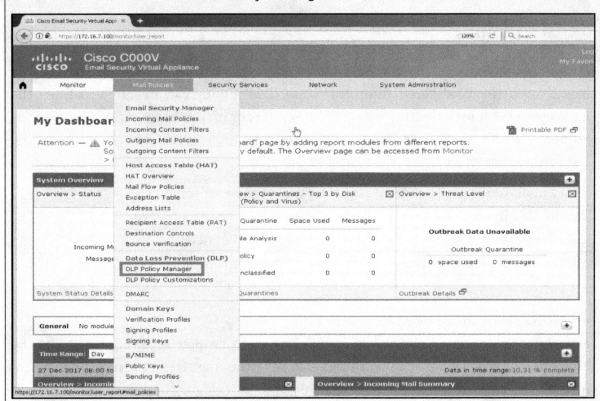

Figure 1-57

2. Click **Add DLP Policy.**

3. Click the name of a category to display a list of the available RSA Email DLP policy templates.

4. Click **Add** for the RSA Email DLP policy template that you want to use.

5. You can edit the predefined name & description.

6. Enter a regular expression if required.

7. Apply the DLP policy.

8. In the Severity Settings section:

Choose an action to take for each level of violation severity.

(Optional) Click Edit Scale to adjust the violation severity scale for the policy.

9. **Submit** and commit your changes.

Email Authentication

Cisco Email Security Appliance provide Email Security and protection by supporting verification and authentication. For the verification of incoming mail, Cisco ESA supports

- Sender Policy Framework (SPF)
- Sender ID Framework (SIDF)
- Domain-based Message Authentication
- DomainKeys Identified Mail (DKIM)
- Forged Email Detection.
- Reporting and Conformance (DMARC)

To authenticate outbound mail, Cisco ESA supports DomainKeys and DKIM signing.

Domain Keys

Domain Keys is an Email Authentication at the domain level. These Domain keys are used to validate the emails to be authentic generating form the domain of the corporate network depending upon the DNS record of the domain. Addition of Unique Digital Code offers the benefit of approving and authentication of outgoing emails. These unique digital codes are added in the Email header. Using Public and Private keys, recipient can authenticate the Email.

DomainKeys Identified Mail (DKIM)

DomainKeys Identified Mail (DKIM) is an authentication mechanism for Emails to detect Email spoofing. It allows the receiver of message to check the email, received from a specific domain was indeed authorized by the owner of that domain. This technique is used to prevent forged senders of Email; traditionally Forged sender of Emails are notices in phishing or Email Spamming.

DomainKeys Identified Mail (DKIM) set the domain name with the message by associating with a digital signature. Verification process is carried out by the signer's public key published in the DNS. A valid signature ensures that the email is not modified and coming from the legitimate source. DKIM signatures are not visible for the users. Signatures are affixed or verified by the infrastructure rather than message's sender and recipients.

Enable DomainKey/DKIM Signing

1. Create or Import Private key by Navigating to **Mail Policies > Signing Keys.**

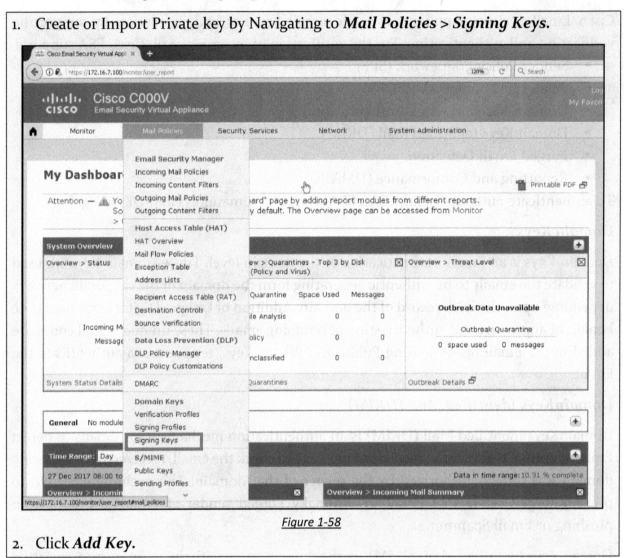

Figure 1-58

2. Click **Add Key.**

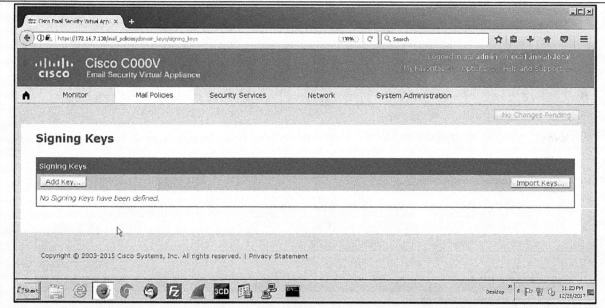

Figure 1-59

Figure 1-59

3. Name the Key.
4. Click **Generate** and select a key size.

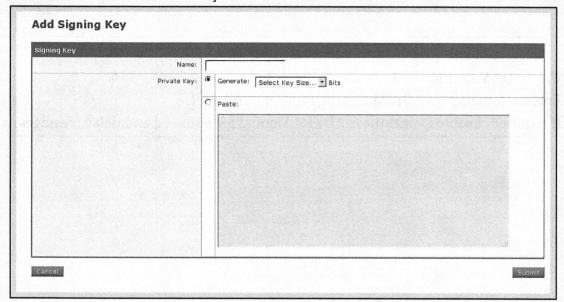

Figure 1-60

5. Click **Submit** and **Commit** changes
6. Create Domain Profile and associate Signing key with the Domain Profile from **Mail Policies > Signing Profiles.**

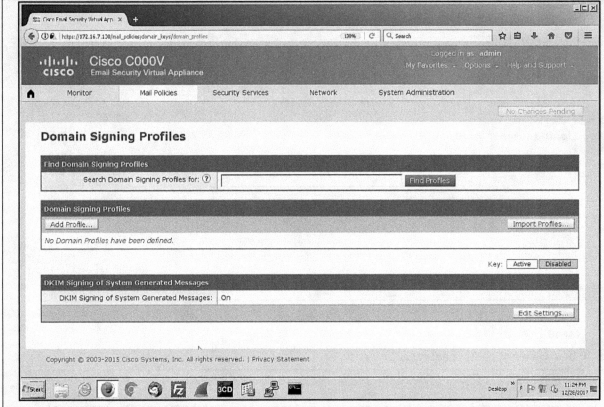

Figure 1-61

7. Create **DNS Text Record.**
8. Enable DomainKeys / DKIM Signing for outbound mail.
9. If required, Enable DomainKeys / DKIM Signing for bounced and delay messages.

Email Authentication flow using DomainKeys and DKIM

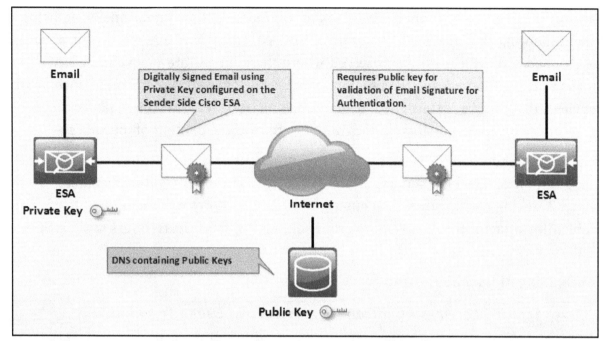

Figure 1-62: Email Authentication Flow

1. Publishing the Public Key to the DNS.
2. Loading Private key in the outbound Mail Transfer Agent (MTA).
3. Email from an authorized user with in the domain is digitally signed with private key.
4. The signature is inserted as a DomainKey or DKIM signature header and the email is transmitted.
5. Receiving Mail Transfer Agent (MTA) extracts the DomainKeys or DKIM signature from the header and the claimed sending domain.
6. The public key is used to determine whether the DomainKeys or DKIM signature was generated with the appropriate private key.

Signing Key

Signing Key is basically the private key that is stored on the Email Security Appliance. Large key size is more secure but they also impact on performance. The Email Security Appliance support the key ranging from 512 bits to 2048 bits. Configuring 768 to 1024 bits' key size are secure and efficient.

Public Key

Public key is the key used for authentication of the Emails. This Public key is inserted while configuring the DNS Text Record. Comparing the Signed Certificates from the Public key ensures that the email is from Actual Sender or it is modified.

Message Tracking

Tacking Message feature offers the tracking of Email traffic. Traditionally, it helps in troubleshooting the Emails which are not delivered. Using Message tracking, emails that are stopped somewhere can be observed where these emails are blocked. Observing the Emails that are blocked due to containing viruses, or blocked due to compliance of DLP policies etc., can be determined using Tracking feature. Tracking feature does not compromise on confidentiality, it does not offer to read the content of messages.

Message Tracking offers tracking for the messages that are transmitted after the configuration of Tracking service. If Message Filter or Content Filter is enabled on the device, Tracking result shows Attachment information, therefore One of the filter is must enabled for attachment details. Similarly enabling log file feature offers storing Subject headers.

Configuring Message Tracking

1. Go to *Security Services* > *Centralized Services* > *Message Tracking*

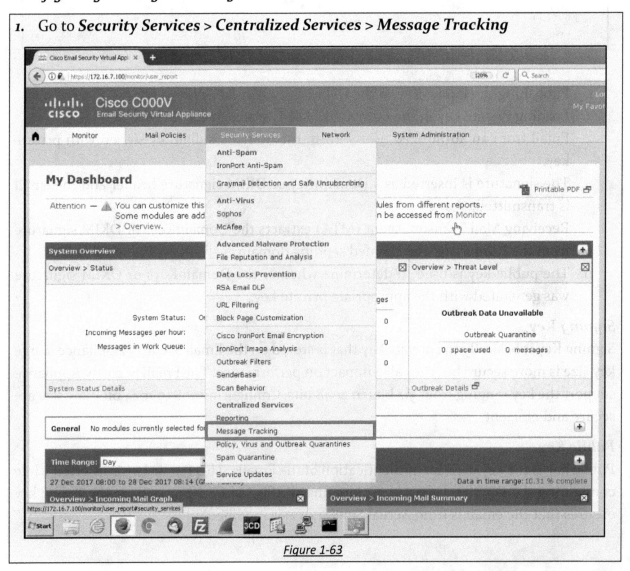

Figure 1-63

2. Select *Enable Message Tracking*

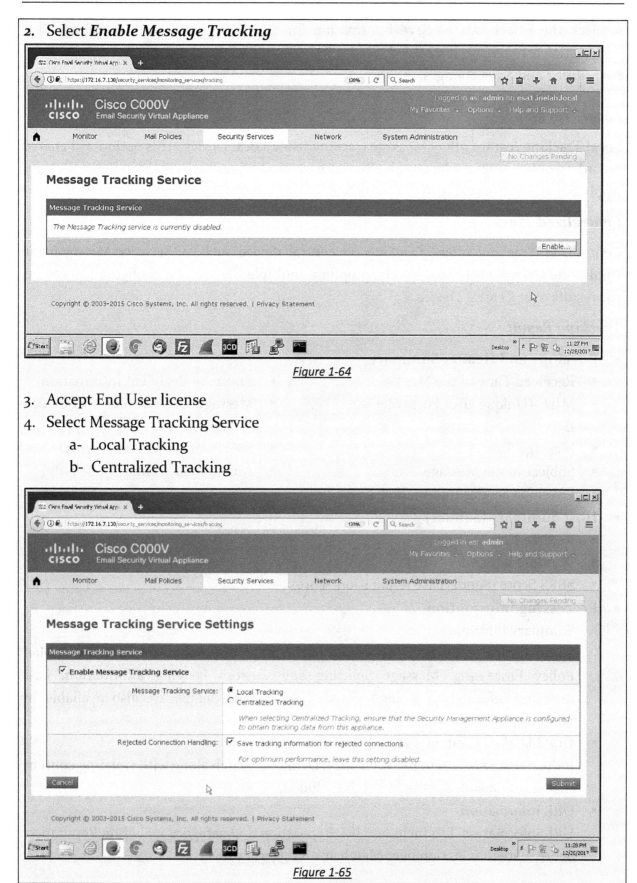

Figure 1-64

3. Accept End User license
4. Select Message Tracking Service
   a- Local Tracking
   b- Centralized Tracking

Figure 1-65

5. Tick the Check box to Save information for rejected connection if required. Best Practice is to remain it disabled.
6. **Submit** and **Save** changes.

Local Tracking

Local Tracking feature offers Message tracking using Local Device. This option will enable recording of tracking results on same device such as configuring over Cisco Email Security Appliance enable recording over Cisco ESA.

Centralized Tracking

Centralized Tracking offers Tracking on central device such as Security Management Appliance. Using Centralized Tracking option, multiple ESA can be configured to record the results over Central Device.

Tracking Result

- **Envelope and Header Summary**
  - Received Time of the Message
  - MID (Unique IronPort Message ID)
  - Message Size
  - Subject of the Message
  - Envelope Sender Information
  - Envelope Recipient Information
  - Message ID Header (RFC 822 Header)
  - SMTP Authenticated User ID
  - Attachment (Name of File only)
- **Host Summary (Sender)**
  - Reverse DNS Hostname
  - IP Address (Sender Host)
  - SBRS Score (SenderBase Reputation Score)
- **Processing Information**
  - Summary Information

    Summary Information contains Logs of the Status Events, information about Mail Policy Processing, Message Splitting and Custom Logging information. Last recorded information is highlighted. If delivered, details are also available in Summary information.
  - DLP Matched Content Tab

    If the message is caught by DLP Policy, Details of Match along with violating content that is responsible for the Match is included.
  - URL Information

    URL information Tab includes URL Reputation and category including Reputation Score, Category, Action over Match and Triggering URL.

Mind Map

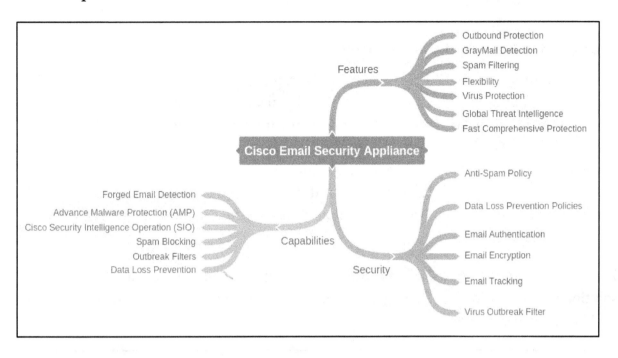

Chapter 2: Network Threat Defense

Evolution of Next Generation Firewalls

Over the Internet, advanced and more sophisticated viruses and malwares are launched with faster propagation capabilities. Traditionally, firewalls are not enough to secure and are less capable in protecting corporate network from application layer vulnerabilities. Evolution of Application layer threats results in the loss of visibility and control. It the great challenge to keep the corporate network secure. Best effort in protecting the corporate network for restoring Application Control and Visibility and keep the network secure is by deploying fully integrated Next-Generation Solution instead of deployment of Single Purpose Security Device.

Basically, Next-Generation Firewalls (NGFW) are the highly focused integrated Security solution which provide Controlling and Protection of Applications from Advanced, highly sophisticated attacks.

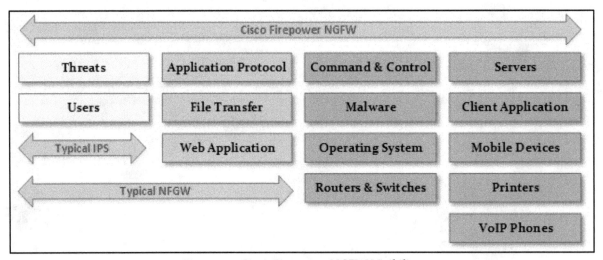

Figure 2-1: Cisco Firepower NGFW Visibility

Cisco Firepower Next-Generation Firewall is the first fully integrated, Threat focused, Next-generation firewall. NGFW keeps user secure, mitigates against advanced threats in rapid responsive time. Cisco Firepower 4100 Series also provide threat-focused NGFW security solution for Internet edge and high-performance environments. It delivers enhanced security responsively with a precise footprint. Cisco Firepower Management Centre offers unified management, Including Cisco Firepower NGFW, Cisco Firepower Next-Generation Intrusion Prevention System and Cisco Advanced Malware Protection. Through Management Centre, management of firewall to control application, investigation and remediation action for malware outbreaks with ease can be done.

Features and Benefits of NGFW

- **Unified Solution**
  - Visibility
  - Management
  - Tacking
  - Record
  - Remediation Action
- **Scalability**
  - Central Management
  - Role Based Management
  - Policy Inheritance
- **Performance and Density Optimization**
  - 10-Gbps and 40-Gbps interfaces
  - Up to 80-Gbps Throughput
  - Low Latency
- **Multi-Service Security**
  - Next-Generation IPS (NGIPS)
  - Application Visibility & Control (AVC)
  - Cisco Advanced Malware Protection (AMP)
  - Radware DefensePro DDoS
  - ASA
  - Third Party Solutions

Cisco Next-Generation Firewall (NGFW) Security Services

Application Awareness

Evolution of Application and Traditional Firewalls

The basic purpose of deploying firewall in a network is to control the traffic between the secure, trusted network such as Private network or Corporate LAN and the untrusted networks such as public Network or the internet. Common and traditional firewalls offer Port-based or packet level filtering and Stateful inspection. These firewalls are easy to deploy and configure. These are inexpensive and offers good throughput.

Port based firewalls requires Source or Destination IP address and Port Information (TCP/UDP) in order to filter the packet from the incoming traffic and determine whether to proceed or deny the packets in case of compliance of conditions. These firewalls only inspect fist few bytes of the header of the Packet to determine Application Protocol.

Evolution of internet not only enhance the services by offering efficient and increased performance and productivity to users which may be accessing through the Public internet or connected through a secure trusted network. These enhanced services include the evolution in Application by launching new generation of Application which are used by various users, personally and for business. These Application not only offers services but also increase the risk of security and threats in term of data loss, using Non-standard Ports, Port hopping, and tunnelling

Classification of Application

Applications functioning with in the network are playing important role in the productivity of an organization. These applications cannot just have classified as good & bad application according to the Risk and Advantages ratio. For example, an application offers low risks as compared to rewards offers by the application can be classified as Good application. Whereas some of the application lies in between them.

Using Applications including Social Media Applications within the corporate network for any purpose like promotions, sales and other reasons may increase production and benefits for the organization. While using the Application, the user may not understand how this application is being used against the organization like for governing purpose. Data loss can also propagate threats into the corporate network. Completely or blindly trusting an application, even on the applications that are classified as good, is not a good approach. Blocking the entire application is also an inappropriate action.

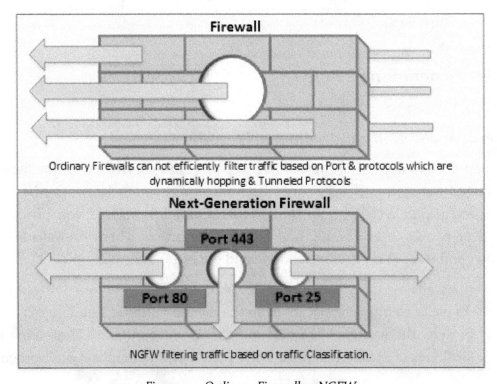

Figure 2-2: Ordinary Firewall vs NGFW

New Generation Applications are designed to offer high availability and performance. These Applications can adjust their communication dynamically to offer high availability from anywhere. The key features that these applications use are:

- **Port hopping**
  Port and protocol using by these applications can be dynamically allocated between end users.

- **Non-Standard ports**
  Application may use Non-Standard Ports instead of using Standard Ports such as any Application using non-standard instead of using Port 80 for HTTP.

- **Tunnelling**
  Application may be tunnelled within the service such as Tunnelling within running HTTP.

- **Masking**
  Application may hide traffic within SSL Encryption.

Application Identification using Next-Generation Firewall

Next Generation Firewalls offers the solution of security of the corporate network from these applications. The next generation firewall classify the traffic and offers visibility and control over the Application. The next generation firewalls are capable of:

- Identification of Application independent of Port or protocol using and SSL encryption.
- Application granular visibility and control, policy based controlling including individual functions over applications.
- Identification of users without false positive result using user-identity information.
- Real time Application layer protection.
- Integration Option.
- High Performance with Multi-gigabit support.

Identification of application using next generation firewalls includes the following key components:

- **Application Protocol Identification**
  NGFW identify the Protocol in use by the application. If encrypted traffic is detected such as SSL packet is catcher, packet will be decrypted for inspection including Policy filtering and Anti-Virus scanning. After analysis, packet will be re-encrypted.

- **Application Tunnelled Protocol identification**
  NGFW can detect the Protocol in use by the application is the only protocol or the application is masking another protocol with the upper protocol.

- **Application Signatures**

Application signatures such as context based signature offers identification of application regardless of port and protocols.

Access Control Policies

Access Control policies are configured to control access to the network resources. These Control policies consists of a set of rules including pre-defined and custom conditions. Traffic is inspected according to the criteria of the policy for compliance. If multiple rules are configured, the first matching rule entry will be applied on the traffic. Encrypted traffic can also have inspected for virus and threats. Default action apply the default action over the traffic with no match found. Traffic with no match can either be permit, deny or an IPS inspection can be applied over it. Control Policy can be configured in the network where

- Policy is to be configured for attributes like IP address of source and destination, Protocol, Ports as well as interfaces (Security Zone)
- Policy is to be configured for specific application. Rule can be associated over Category of Application, Tag and type such as Client Application.
- Policy is to be configured for destination URL. URL can be configured using Pre-defined URL Categories and using Reputation score.
- Policy is to be configured associated with the specific user or group of User.

Access control Policy include the following filtering option that can be configured as rules for traffic matching certain condition:

- Application Filtering
- URL Filtering
- Reputation Filtering
- File Filtering

Application Filtering

Application filtering can be done by using Access Control Policy which identify and filter the specific application running within the traffic of corporate network along with various other applications. Access Control Policy detect the particular application, it become easy to block specific application without blocking other application. Application filtering also offers granular control over some application by blocking features of the Application instead of blocking the complete application. For example, Blocking Chat or Upload option in any application.

URL Filtering

URL filtering offers controlling of websites. Specific URL categories can be filtered and access can be controlled for websites based on their reputation score. URL Filtering License offers URL Filtering using Pre-Defined Categories of URL and Reputation based filtering.

Without License of URL filtering, Manual Filtering can be configured which requires manual addition of individual URL or group of URL's.

As defined above, URL Filtering requires URL Filtering license. This License URL Filtering can be done using:

- **Category based Filtering**
  1. *Permit or Deny traffic by Filtering URL Category*

There is the list of categories in which every website lies. URL Filtering can be done by using this list. For example, www.google.com is associated with the Search engine category whereas www.facebook.com or www.linkedin.com are from the Social Networking Category. Filtration can be applied over these categories. URL Filtering Profile with specified action over each URL category associated with the Access Control Policy can filter the traffic that match the policy.

  2. *Filter Traffic by URL Category for Policy Enforcement*

Enforcement of a policy on a specific category of website can be done by adding category as matching criteria or policy rule.

- **Reputation based Filtering**

For the security concern, a website may filter using Reputation based URL Filtering by comparing the Reputation score of the website. This reputation score ranges for level 1 as High Risk to Level 5 as Well-Known website. Reputation filtering compare the reputation data from Cisco SenderBase. Cisco SenderBase is a global repository which records reputation. When any Host is involved in malicious or potentially harmful activities, it lowers the reputation of that host. Comparing the information from Cisco SenderBase, by Reputation filtering supported device can perform certain action and proceed to the next level of inspection and filtering. URL with lower reputation can be configured to block.

File Filtering

Intrusion Scanning, Malware Inspection and File Policy are the combined security feature which offers the last line of defense. After intrusion and file inspection, the traffic proceeds toward the destination. Intrusion Policies offer Intrusion prevention whereas File Policy offers File Control and Advanced Malware Protection. This filtration process filters the traffic by examination for intrusion, Restricted Files, Virus and Malwares etc. Configuring the File filtering associating with Access Control Policy ensures the inspection of traffic for the File Policy.

Traffic Redirection

The Cisco Adaptive Security Appliance Firepower Module which is also known as ASA SFR offers Next-Generation firewall services on ASA including Next Generation Intrusion

Prevention System (NGIPS), URL Filtering, Advanced Malware Protection (AMP) and Application Visibility and Control (AVC). SFR module can be use in Routed or Transparent mode.

ASA Firepower Module Options

- **Inline Mode**

In the Network Security Deployment where ASA Firepower module is deployed in Inline Mode, the actual traffic is directed to the ASA Firepower module. ASA Firepower Module apply the Next-Generation Firewall services over the traffic and take action specified by the associating policies. After processing, traffic is forwarded to the ASA for delivering to the destination.

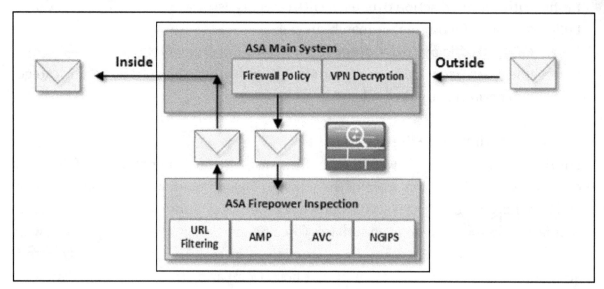

Figure 2-3: Inline Mode

- **Inline Tap Monitor-Only Mode**

Inline Tap Monitor-Only deployment does not take original packet for ASA Firepower module as in Inline mode, a copy of traffic is forwarded to the ASA Firepower module. This copy is only for SFR module, it does not send back to ASA as Inline Mode deployment does. Inline Tap Monitor-Only Mode offers visibility of the processes, processed by the SFR module without affecting the network performance. If the traffic matches any condition according to the access policies, certain action is applied.

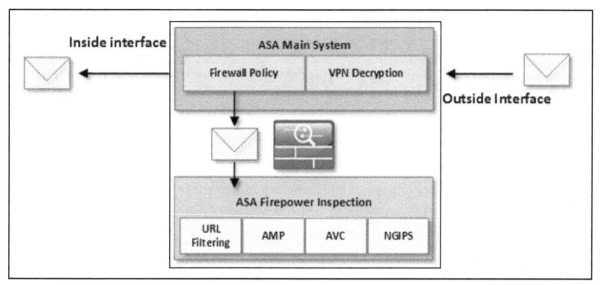

Figure 2-4: Inline Tap Monitor-Only Mode

- **Passive Monitor-Only Mode**

  ASA Firepower also offers operation in Passive Monitor-Only mode. In this Passive Monitoring Mode, there is no impact on the traffic and over performance of the network. Passive Monitoring acts as Intrusion Detection System which only monitor, detect and shows the results indicating what has done with the traffic. Traffic is forwarded to the Firepower Module directly without any ASA processing. When passive mode receives the traffic, it inspects the traffic according to the access policies and take action associated with the matched condition and show result. Using the analysis report, requirement of inline deployment can be decided. In Passive Monitoring, neither ASA nor ASA Firepower module forward the traffic to any destination.

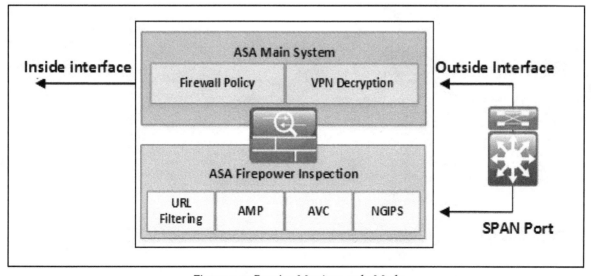

Figure 2-5: Passive Monitor-only Mode

ASA Firepower Default Network Parameters

Parameter	Default Values
Management IP address	System Software Image 192.168.45.45/24
	Boot image : 192.168.8.8/24
Gateway	System Software Image : none
	Boot image : 192.168.8.1/24
SSH / Session Username	admin
Password	System Software Image : Sourcefire
	Boot image : Admin123

Table 2-1: ASA Firepower Default Parameters

Redirecting Traffic to ASA Firepower Module

Service Policy is required in order to redirect the traffic to Inline or Inline Tap Monitor Mode Only. For redirection of traffic to Passive Monitor-Only mode, Traffic redirection interface is required. Configuration steps for both Inline Modes and Passive mode are as follows:

1. **Configure Traffic Redirection to Inline / Inline Tap Monitor-Only Modes**
   Service policy offers redirection of traffic to the ASA Firepower module. If there is any active service policy configured redirecting to IPS or any other module, remove that service policy. After redirection to the firepower module, Access Control Policies, Access rules and respective actions are applied before forwarding the traffic to delivery.

Traffic Redirection Configuration

1) Go to **Configuration > Firewall > Service Policy Rules**

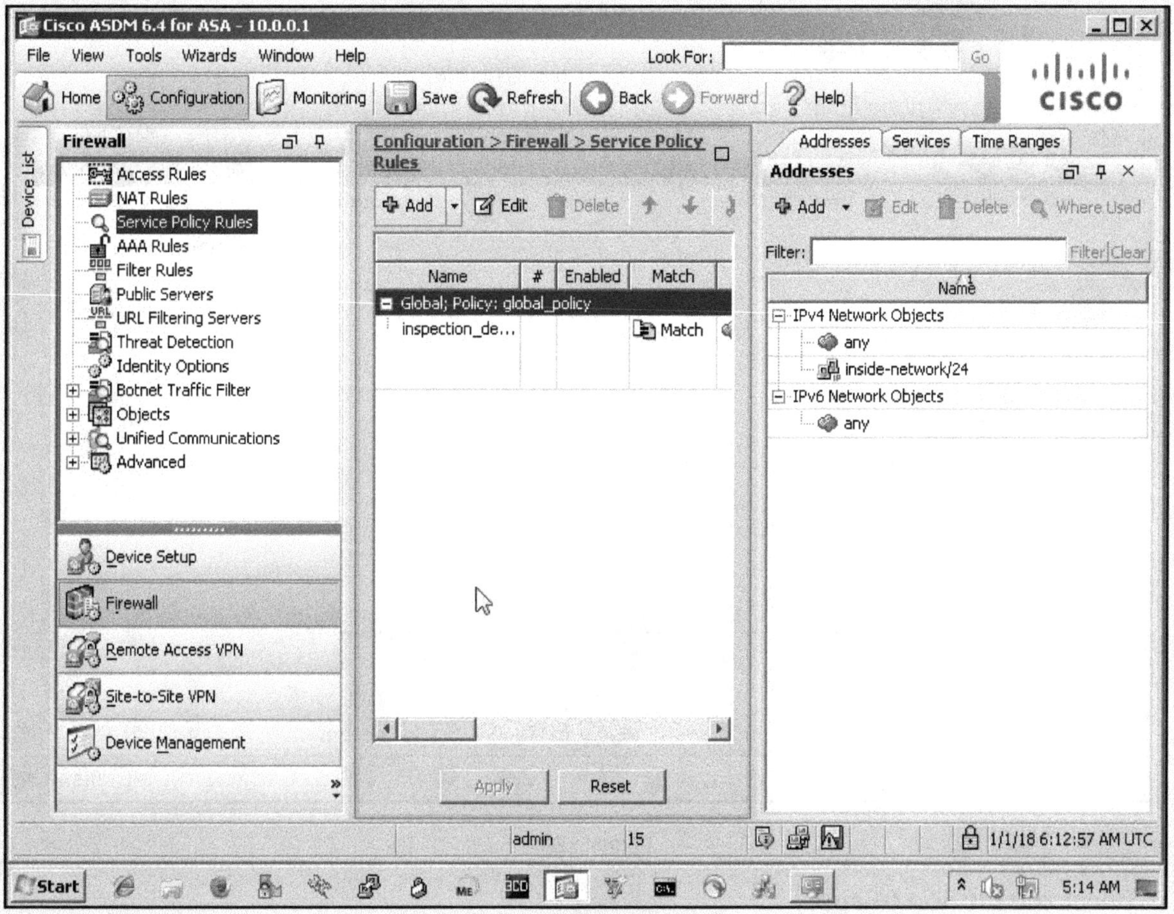

Figure 2-6

2) Select **Add > Add Service Policy Rule**

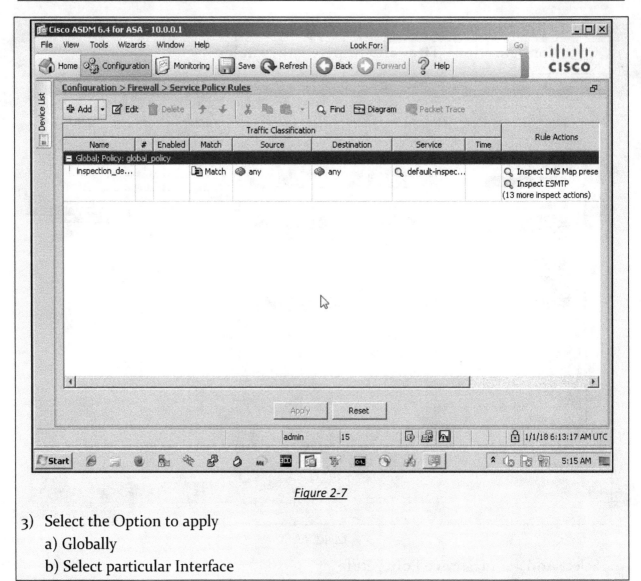

Figure 2-7

3) Select the Option to apply
   a) Globally
   b) Select particular Interface

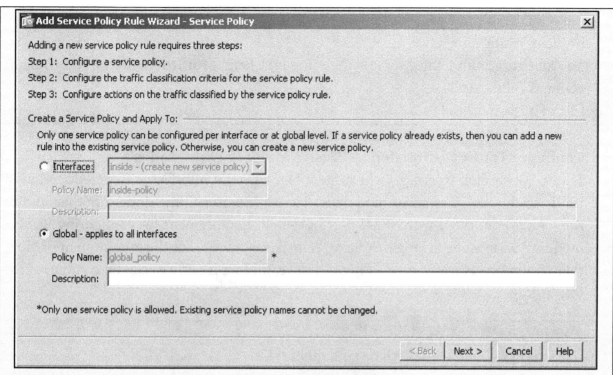

Figure 2-8

4) Configure Traffic match. Configuring Any Traffic allow redirection of all traffic to module.

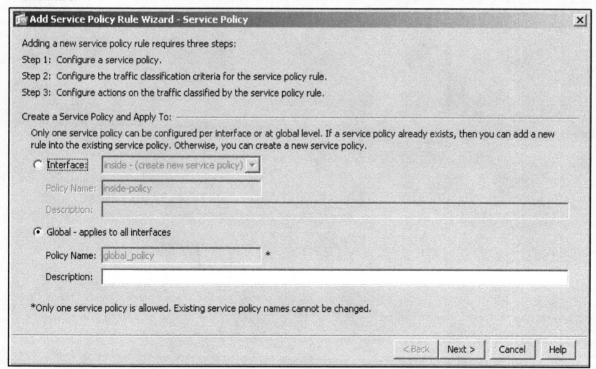

Figure 2-9

5) Go to **ASA Firepower Inspection** tab on **Rule Action** page
6) Tick the check box **Enable ASA Firepower for this traffic Flow**
7) Select the Option for **ASA Firepower Card Fails area**

> a) Permit Traffic
> b) Close Traffic
> 8) To Configure Inline Tap Monitor-Only mode, Check **Monitor-Only** option. Default action is Inline Mode.
> 9) Click Finish and Apply

2. **Configure Traffic Redirection to Passive Monitor-Only Modes**

   Traffic Forwarding Interface (which must be a Physical interface) offers redirection of traffic to the ASA Firepower module in Passive Monitor-Only Mode. Another End of the Link is connected with SPAN port of switch. Requirement for configuring Passive mode is ASA must be in Single Context, transparent mode. For the requirement of More than 1 interface as traffic forwarding interface, up to 4 interfaces can be configured for forwarding.

Configure ASA Traffic Forwarding Interface
ASA(config)# interface *[interface-type-number]*
ASA(config)# no nameif
ASA(config)# traffic-forward sfr monitor-only
ASA(config)# no shutdown

Mind Map

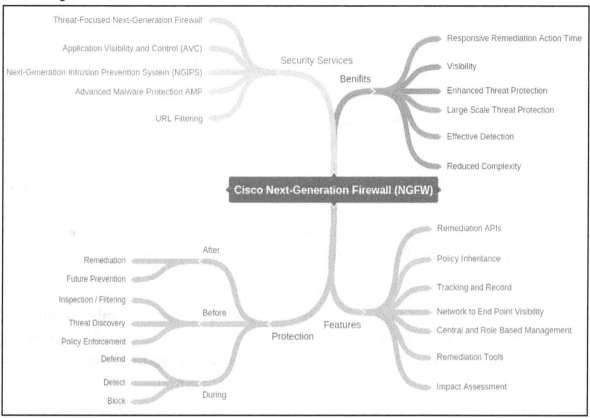

Cisco Advanced Malware Protection (AMP)

Introduction to Advanced Malware Protection (AMP)

Advanced Malware Protection (AMP) is the one of the major components of Next-Generation Security deployment. Cisco AMP provide security not only by detection and protection of threats but also mitigating the impact of that attack on the network. Cisco AMP offers the detection of various, advanced, large scale malicious programs, AMP enables to detect them, block and continuously inspect against the presence of malwares.

Cisco AMP offers continuous monitoring and Detection against the threats, malwares and perform immediate action retrospectively. Flexibility of device type offers capability to support MAC, Linux, Android, iOS, Windows and Servers etc. It records activity to track the malware spreading and ability to scope the compromise. Correlation of discrete events, Integration with global threat intelligence strengthen the network defense capabilities.

Comprehensive Global Threat Intelligence

Cisco Advanced Malware Protection deployment with full integrated solution including public cloud offers comprehensive global threat intelligence, malware intelligence feed from sophisticated threat analysis engines including wide collection of real time virus

outbreaks and malware information along with deep visibility, wide footprint and capability to take certain action according to the nature of threat level across various security devices.

Static and Dynamic Malware Analysis

Anti-Virus and Malware scanning can perform offline causing system based detection of malicious activities scanning and Monitoring the traffic. This efficient scanning engine can perform local IoC scanning and traffic flow monitoring. This anti-virus engine ensures the capability of endpoint protection from virus and malwares by offering an extremely sophisticated sandboxing environment where examination, inspection and testing of threat can be achieved for unidentified Zero-day threats. For even more achievement of comprehensive security, AMP can be integrated with Threat Grid which offers not only sandboxing but Static and Dynamic analysis features using behavioural indicators.

AMP Architecture

The AMP cloud that is also known as AMP Private Cloud contains number of analysing tools and technologies for the detection of malware in within the traffic. AMP Cloud also includes the Threat Grid analysis solution which offers advanced sandboxing and threat intelligence features to be a unified solution for protecting from malwares. Threat Grid Combines Static and dynamic analysis of Malwares with the threat intelligence and real time behavioural analysis. Threat intelligence from other Cisco security products, third-party relationships and Public Security Cloud is also sent to the AMP cloud.

Cisco Collective Security Intelligence (CSI)

The Talos Security Intelligence and Research Group (Talos) is a Security intelligence research that is feed up with the leading sophisticated threat intelligence. TALOS delivers threat intelligence to Public Security Cloud like Cisco Collective Security Intelligence (CSI) ecosystem that can integrate with Advanced Malware Protection Private Cloud (AMP Cloud) and delivers intelligence of known and emerging threats to the AMP Cloud. Talos has the official regulations for Snort.org, ClamAV and SenderBase.org. These platforms are managed with expertise, reverse engineering, Threat vulnerability triage, malwares and virus investigation and intelligence.

Talos contributes its threat intelligence information to Cisco Collective Security Intelligence (CSI) ecosystem. Cisco CSI is a publically Cloud-hosted engine that is shared across multiple security solutions like Cisco products such as Cisco AMP, Cisco WSA, Cisco ESA and other security appliances and provides enhanced security solution with protection and efficacy. In addition, CSI is updated by intelligence infrastructure, telemetry, public and private feeds and the open source communities.

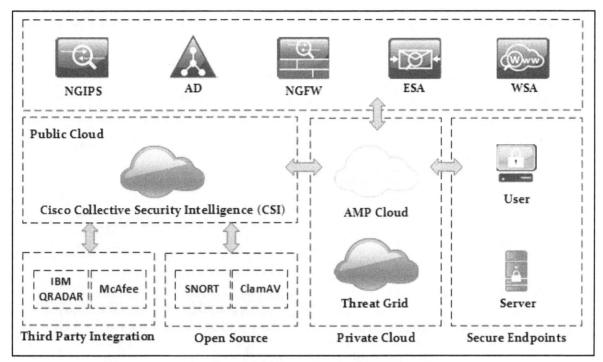

Figure 2-10: Advanced Malware Protection AMP Architecture

Cisco AMP Private Cloud Virtual Appliance

Cisco AMP Private Cloud Virtual Appliance is an on-premises Solution that delivers advanced malware protection services along with large scale data analytics, continuous and real-time analytics, and security intelligence which is stored locally. In the deployment scenario where corporate network requires privacy to restrict the use of a public cloud as Public Cloud offers File Scanning and other features. The Cisco Advanced Malware Protection (AMP) Private Cloud Virtual Appliance is the alternative security solution. In Private Cloud deployment scenario, AMP Private Cloud not only satisfies privacy requirements, but also provides advanced malware protection of network and endpoint.

Protection against the upcoming, advanced and emerging threats require a powerful security solution that that is capable to protect the network beyond the detection of threat and remediation actions. Detection of threat before allowing it to access the network and remediation action and scoping the compromise is not enough to rely on. Cisco AMP offers advanced capabilities which offers visibility, Control and Remediation over large scale with advanced intelligence to detect, block, examine the track the record with scalability.

Cisco AMP Private Cloud is the highly secure alternate of Public Cloud Security solution. It not only meets privacy and other organization's policies, if it finds something suspicious, it can get intelligence report from Public Cloud-hosted engine such as Cisco Collective Security Intelligence (CSI) public cloud without sharing personal information's, it sends only anonymized SHA256 information. Cisco Collective Security Intelligence (CSI) public

cloud will update the AMP private cloud with the intelligence report that will be stored locally for future use.

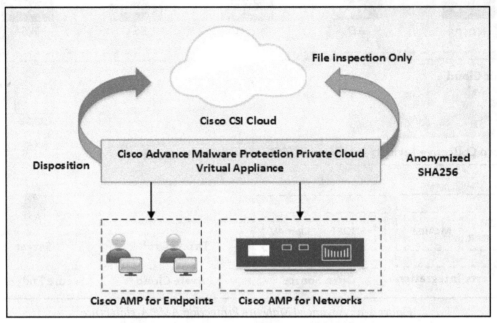

Figure 2-11: AMP Private Cloud with CSI Cloud

Cisco AMP Threat Grid

AMP Threat Grid can be deployed as a cloud-based solution such as Virtually deployed on Physical Server or cloud hosted server or as On-premises solution by Threat Grid Appliance. Cisco Advanced Malware Protection Threat Grid offers the unified solution that includes static results and dynamic malware analysis reports with threat intelligence. Immediate, detailed information that protect corporate network from malwares including Real-time behavioural analytics and threat intelligence integration with existing security technologies, enhanced and strengthen protection against known and unknown attacks.

Cisco AMP Threat Grid offers in-depth visibility for monitoring, controlling and Protecting from malwares. The key benefits from Cisco AMP Threat Grid are:
- Precise and accurate identification of threats and attacks
- Real time intelligence with context-rich security analytics.
- Capability to handle large scale of threats using Cloud Services.
- Enhanced performance with efficacy by integration with other engines.
- Support custom threat intelligence.
- Support third-party security intelligence.

AMP Threat Grid can also examine the suspicious behaviour of the traffic flow in the corporate network with the help of up to 450 behavioural indicators. Cisco AMP Threat Grid along with AMP Cloud and Public Cloud, combined solution provides more accurate, precise and context-rich analytics.

Public & Private Cloud Comparison

Feature	Cisco AMP Private Cloud Virtual Appliance	Cisco CSI Public Cloud
File and Device Trajectory	yes	yes
Threat Root Cause	yes	yes
Cloud Indication and Alerting	yes	yes
Simple and Advanced Custom Detection	yes	yes
Retrospective alerting	yes	yes
File analysis and Scan		yes

Table 2-02: AMP Public & Private Cloud Comparison

AMP Endpoint Deployment

Deployment Options

Product Name	Details
Cisco AMP for Endpoints	Protect Windows, Macs, Linux systems, and Android mobile devices using AMP's lightweight connector. AMP for Endpoints can also be launched from AnyConnect v4.1.
Cisco AMP for Networks	Deploy AMP as a network-based solution integrated into Cisco Firepower NGIPS security appliances.
Cisco AMP on Firewalls and ASA with FirePOWER Services	Deploy AMP capabilities integrated into the Cisco NGFW or ASA Adaptive Security Appliance firewall.
Cisco AMP Private Cloud Virtual Appliance	Deploy AMP as an on-premises solution built specifically for organizations with high-privacy requirements that restrict using a public cloud.
Cisco AMP on ESA, or WSA	For Cisco Email Security Appliance (ESA) or Web Security Appliance (WSA), AMP capabilities can be turned on to provide retrospective capabilities and malware analysis.
Cisco AMP for Meraki MX	Deploy AMP as part of the Meraki MX Security Appliance for cloud-based simplified security management with advanced threat capabilities.
Cisco Threat Grid	Threat Grid is integrated with Cisco AMP for enhanced malware analysis. It can also be deployed as a standalone advanced malware analysis and threat intelligence solution, in the cloud or on an appliance.

Table 2-03: Cisco AMP Deployment Options

Software Requirements

Deployment	Software Requirement
Cisco AMP for Endpoints on Apple iOS	MDM supervised iOS version 11
Cisco AMP for Endpoints on Android mobile devices	Android version 2.1 and later
Cisco AMP for Endpoints	Microsoft Windows XP with Service Pack 3 or later
	Microsoft Windows Vista with Service Pack 2 or later
	Microsoft Windows 7
	Microsoft Windows 8 and 8.1
	Microsoft Windows 10
	Microsoft Windows Server 2003
	Microsoft Windows Server 2008
	Microsoft Windows Server 2012
	Mac OS X 10.7 and later
	Linux Red Hat Enterprise 6.5, 6.6, 6.7, 6.8, 7.2, and 7.3
	Linux CentOS 6.4, 6.5, 6.6, 6.7, 6.8, 7.2 and 7.3

Table 2-04: Cisco AMP Endpoint Software Requirement

Downloading Connector for Endpoint

To download Endpoint Connector, go to Download Connector Page. From there, Endpoint connector package can be downloaded. By copying the URL, the installer package can be offered at any sharing location or deployed via management software. URL can be forwarded to local and remote users for download and manual installation.

AMP Connector of Android Endpoints

AMP for Android Endpoints can be deployed by downloading the android application, sending the link to download application to android users. An activation code will be required for function. Download the APK file or copy the download link.

1. Download the "**FireAMP Mobile**" android Application.
2. Accept the End User License
3. Enter the Activation Code and Name for identification of your device

Figure 2-12: FireAMP Android Application

4. Accept the terms,
5. After accepting, Initial Scan will start, Yellow or Red indication is for Warning or Threat alert respectively. Green will show secured status.

Figure 2-13: FireAMP Android Application

AMP Connector of Windows Endpoints

AMP deployment for Windows Endpoint requires the selection of group. It will show the Connector version which will download according to the policy. It will also show if any of

the connector requires an update. It will also notify how many of the Endpoint computer requires reboot after updating of connector version.

Flash Scan option offers examination of the current processes running if it is enabled, it should be performed as recommended on each installation. The default action is to download a redistributable installer that downloads a 46 MB policy.xml file containing 32 and 64-bit installers. For large scaled Endpoints, this file can be placed in a convenient location or deployed via management tool.

To deploy using management tools such as Microsoft System Centre Configuration Manager (SCCM), go to the Properties option of the AMP Endpoint Connector Installer and Select "Allow users to interact with this program" option.

1. AMP deployment for Mac Endpoints, Similar procedure has to be followed.
2. Select the Group for Drop down menu.
3. Check/Uncheck Flash Scan if Flash Scan is required during installation process.
4. Check/Uncheck Redistributable Installer Option.

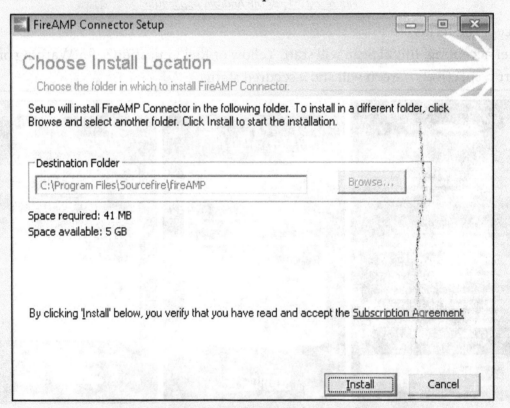

Figure 2-14: AMP Endpoint Windows Installer

Install the Endpoint Windows Installer in desired destination folder.

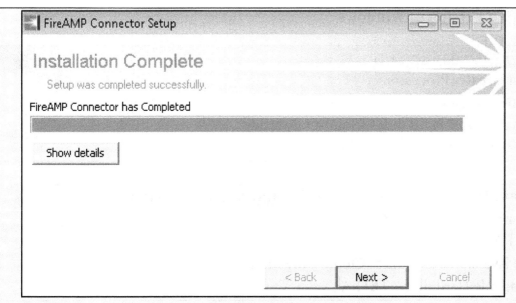

Figure 2-15: AMP Endpoint Windows Installing

Installation of Windows Endpoint connector.

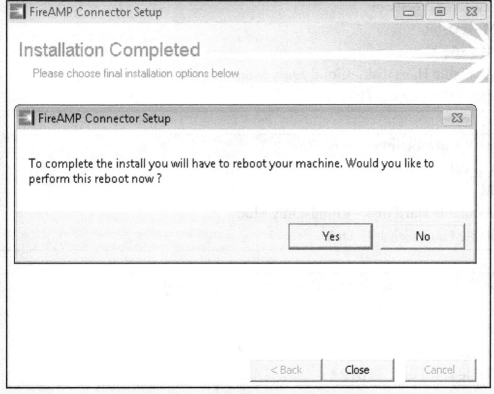

Figure 2-16: AMP Endpoint Windows Installing

Reboot the PC after installation.

Supported Version of Windows

Microsoft Windows 7
1 GHz or Greater Processor
1 GB RAM
650 MB Available Hard disk - Cloud-Only Mode
1 GB Available Hard disk – TETRA

Microsoft Windows 8 / 8.1 (Endpoint Connector 3.1.2 or later)
1 GHz or Greater Processor
512 MB RAM
650 MB Available Hard disk - Cloud-Only Mode
1GB Available Hard disk – TETRA

Microsoft Windows 10 (Endpoint Connector 4.3.0 or later)
1 GHz or Greater Processor
1 GB RAM - x32-bit
2 GB RAM - x64-bit
650 MB Available Hard disk - Cloud-Only Mode
1GB Available Hard disk – TETRA

Microsoft Windows Server 2008 R2
2 GHz or Greater Processor
2 GB RAM
650 MB Available Hard disk - Cloud-Only Mode
1GB Available Hard disk – TETRA

Microsoft Windows Server 2012 (Connector 3.1.9 or later)
2 GHz or Greater Processor
2 GB RAM
650 MB Available Hard disk - Cloud-Only Mode
1GB Available Hard disk - TETRA

AMP Connector of Mac Endpoints

AMP deployment for Mac Endpoints, Similar procedure has to be followed.

1. Select the Group for Drop down menu.
2. Select the if Flash Scan is required during installation process.
3. Pkg file will download, to install the Endpoints or Download link can be copied.

This pkg file is of 5 MB containing policy.xml file.

Step to Configure MAC Installer
1. Right-Click on the PKG file and Select Open
2. Click Continue to Proceed
3. Read Software License agreement and Click Continue
4. Click Agree to accept terms and agreement
5. Select Destination drive for installation (Installation requires 14 MB free space and 50 MB space for signature files)
6. Click Continue to proceed
7. Click Install to begin
8. Enter your password when prompted
9. Accept incoming network connection to get update form Cisco Cloud
10. Click Finish to complete the installation.

Supported Version of Windows

Apple OS X 10.8
2 GB RAM
65 MB Available Hard Disk

Apple OS X 10.9
2 GB RAM
65 MB Available Hard Disk

Apple OS X 10.10 (AMP Mac Connector 1.0.6 or later)
2 GB RAM
65 MB Available Hard Disk

Apple OS X 10.11 (AMP Mac Connector 1.0.7 or later)
2 GB RAM
65 MB Available Hard Disk

Apple OS X 10.12 (AMP Mac Connector 1.2.4 or later)
2 GB RAM
65 MB Available Hard Disk

Apple OS X 10.13 (AMP Mac Connector 1.5.0 or later)
2 GB RAM
65 MB Available Hard Disk

AMP Connector of Linux Endpoints

AMP deployment for Linux Endpoints, Similar procedure has to be followed.

1. Select the Group for Drop down menu.
2. Select the if Flash Scan is required during installation process.
3. rpm file will download, to install the Endpoints or Download link can be copied.
4. Download or Copy GPG Public Key required for Product update.

Rpm file is of 16 MB containing policy.xml file, this file can be placed in a convenient location to be accessible for users. Distribution option also offers for Red Hat Enterprise Linux (RHEL) or CentOS v6.x or 7.x.

To install the Linux package, Execute the following command
sudo yum localinstall [rpm file name] -y
Compare the GPG key at **/opt/cisco/amp/etc/rpm-gpg/RPM-GPG-key-cisco-amp**
Run the command to import the key
sudo rpm --import /opt/cisco/amp/etc/rpm-gpg/RPM-GRP-Key-cisco-amp

Cisco AMP Analysing tools

Indication of Compromise (IoC)

Indication of Compromise feature offers the correlation of intelligence and data received from multiple security events such as detection of intrusion, malware activity detection and other warning and security alerts. These automatic correlation analytics supports the security team for detection, prevention, and analysis to prioritize the threat.

Endpoint IoC's

The Endpoint Indication of Compromise (IoC) is the advanced, enhanced, and efficient scanning tools to analyze the scope of compromise the potential level of threat across endpoints. These Endpoint IoC's are imported from OpenIoC files. These Files are directed to for File properties and System properties. IoC syntax may be used for finding and detection of malicious artefacts or it can be done by sophisticated correlation.

- Cisco Endpoint IoC's are to search for the same file attributes in a single IOC document. AND operation offers the capability to search for more than one attribute

in a document. When requirement is for investigating for multiple attributes like matching for filename like virus.exe and malware.exe

- Similarly, IoC's are capable to match against the combination different object types in an IOC document.
- Capable of combining different Object level attributes in a single IOC document.

File Reputation

Advanced Malware Protection AMP can protect against zero-day and focused file based threats. Cisco AMP Collects the reputation of known files, examine the behaviour of those files which are not yet known to the reputation service. It also keeps inspecting the advanced threats for update of information regarding emerging threats. It also alerts the user when these files have entered in to the network in case when it detects after update of threat intelligence.

The file reputation service is offered by the Public cloud for Collective Security Intelligence powered by TALOS and integrated with a number of engines and third-party platforms. The file analysis service has options for either public or private-cloud. Private cloud as discussed in the solution can be deployed on Virtual Private Cloud Appliance or Virtualize on Server.

The private-cloud file reputation service is offered by AMP Virtual Private Cloud deployed in either "proxy" or "air-gap" mode. Private Cloud only send the File to public Cloud such as Cisco Collective Security Intelligence (CSI) without sharing personal information's. AMP Private Cloud sends only anonymized SHA256 information. Cisco Collective Security Intelligence (CSI) public cloud will perform File reputation analysis and update the AMP private cloud with the intelligence report that will be stored locally for future use.

The private-cloud file analysis service is provided by an on-premises Cisco AMP Threat Grid appliance.

File Trajectory

Cisco AMP offers tracking of files transmitting across the network. Tracking of file shows an isolated view of file trajectory having a visual display of trajectory statistics with respect to time. Trajectory view also includes the information regarding the associated file.

File trajectory is beneficial in terms of determination of the scope of compromise and impact of infection on the network immediately because file trajectory continuously keeps the examination of files. For more precise determination of threats and impact, contextual information such as source and destination systems information involved in the activity are also added.

The following are the sign shown in the file trajectory results:

Figure 2-17: File trajectory Sign

File trajectory can display the following types of file:
- Executable Files
- Archive Files
- Script Files
- Installer Files
- Plain Text Files
- Rich Text Files
- MS Office Files
- MS Cabinet Files
- Adobe Shock Ware Flash
- Portable Document Format PDF

File Trajectory Tracking Results

File trajectory result shows the following information:

Parameters	Information Included
Visibility	Fist Seen Date
	last Seen Date

	Total Number of Observation
Observation	Number of time file is questioned as Source or target file
Entry Point	Fist Location where threat is detected
Created By	File which create the threat
	Number of times Threat is created by that file
File Details	File details include File name, product Information & other details.
Known As	SHA-256 / SHA-1 / MD5 hash of file
Attributes	File type and Size

Table 2-05: File Trajectory Result parameters

Device Trajectory

Device trajectory tool monitors and display the activity of a particular AMP Endpoint connector-deployed Endpoints. Activity includes File tracks, activities of network and connector event including parent processes, remote host connections, unknown files activity. It also offers granular visibility in the event and activities shown by the device trajectory even before and after threat detection and compromise.

Device Trajectory is an enhanced and powerful tool which is capable to scope up to several millions of events. The file, triggering the event, will be cached until it triggers another event.

Device Trajectory Filters

1. **Event Type**

   Describe the Event recorded by AMP Endpoint Connector. Events may include File Events, Network Events and Connector Events.

File Events	Copy, Move, Execution & Other
Network Events	Inbound / Outbound Connections for Local / Remote Users
Connector Events	Policy Update / Scan / Reboot etc.

2. **Event Disposition**

   Event Disposition offers filtration of events based on disposition such as Malicious, Clean or Unknown files.

3. **Event Flag**

   Event Flag offers filtration with respects to the flag such as Warning flag.

4. **File Type**

   File Type filter offers filtration with respect to file type.

Device trajectory can also display the following types of file:
- Executable Files
- Archive Files
- Script Files
- Installer Files
- Plain Text Files
- Rich Text Files
- MS Office Files
- MS Cabinet Files
- Adobe Shock Ware Flash
- Portable Document Format PDF

File Repository

File Repository feature allow the users to test the file they are downloading or user can simply upload the file for additional security audits. File will be downloaded from the Endpoint connector of AMP. File repository examines the file against the threat and malicious activities. File Analysis can be imported for decision support.

File Repository feature offers on the Connectors running the following:
- AMP for Endpoint Windows connector v3.1.9 or later
- AMP for Endpoint MAC connector v1.0.2.6 or later
- AMP for Endpoint Linux connector v1.0.2.261 or later

File Repository State	Function
Requested	When file is requested but connector has not responded
Being Processed	When requested file is under process
Available	When file is available for Download
Failed	When any error occurred during process.

Table 2-06: File Repository States

Threat Root Cause

The Threat Root Cause tool ensures the identification of application and classification into legitimate and rogue applications. Threat root cause is the sophisticated tool that is focused for the identification and detecting the root cause of malwares entering the system. Using the Threat Root Cause Tool shows the default current and last day records. However, you can select date range to see previous records. Records shown by Threat Root Cause include the top 10 software which causes introducing malware into the network.

Prevalence

Prevalence analytics report shows the list of files which have been installed by the endpoints on large scale or executed globally. Normally, large scale execution of an application which may not be a legitimate application is considered as a legitimate application. Prevalence scope the applications which are executed globally which helps estimating the threat executed by small scale known as Low Prevalence Executables. Low Prevalence Executables lists by the lower number of deployment. Results shows File information, Operating System on which file executed. File disposition is shown by the colors Red and Grey indicating Malicious and Unknown file respectively. Clean and Known files are not listed.

Incident Response with Cisco AMP

Cisco offers the advance portfolio for the securing the network from emerging threat, detecting the violation and breaches, along with mitigation techniques and remediation methods to address data and information stolen issues, Trojans, ransomwares and targeted attacks. Cisco offers the mitigation techniques which help in effectively responding to these targeted attacks and large-scale vulnerability that has crossed all security perimeters.

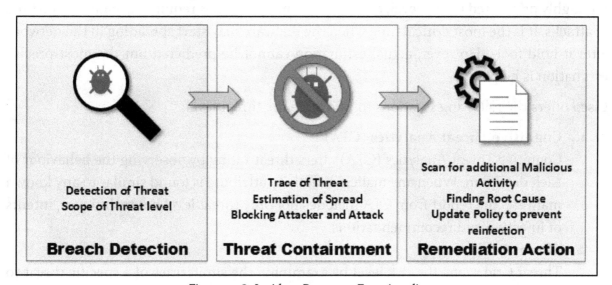

Figure 2-18: Incident Response Functionality

The incident response functionality depends upon the 3 comprehensive steps including:
1. Breach Detection and Prioritization
2. Threat Containment
3. Remediation Action

Breach Detection and Prioritization

The initial and the most challenging step of incident response is to detect the virus, malware or malicious activity in your network because as the famous phrase used in network security environment, "if you can't see it, you can't detect it". The network must be deployed with Cisco Recommended advanced security solution along with necessary integration to detect these emerging threats using deep packet inspection. Examination by using intelligence from various platforms include Collective Security Intelligence, Cisco AMP Virtual Private Cloud, Threat Grid and other third party solution.

Violation may indicate a vulnerability that the attacker has already crossed the security layers and is penetrating in the corporate environment. Breach may potentially infect the systems by encrypting the devices or may impersonate into a legitimate user to steal more information however they may be of an advanced type which information may not be available at security database or a modified form of malware. If the attacks are a most advanced type, it is detected through generic analytics based detection system.

When a malicious activity has been detected before further inspection, priority of the threat is to be determined in order to estimate the potential severity level on the environment. For highly prioritized threat level, an automatic mechanism is required because at the time of attacks, it is the most critical time when the malware may start spreading in the network after it hold foots. However, actual estimation cannot be predicted but the most precise estimation is helpful.

Cisco offers the following solutions to prioritize the threat level:

1. **Cognitive Threat Analytics (CTA)**
   Cognitive Threat Analytics (CTA) offers threat rating by observing the behaviour of each detection. When any malicious activity attribute is found similar to any known malware, the report from CTA includes not only threat level but techniques, intents of infection and recommendations.

2. **Threat Grid**
   Threat Grid scope the risk level by examining the similarities of a specific threat to the previously examined threat of same behaviour or same origin.

3. **AMP for Endpoints**
   AMP for Endpoint keeps record of file activities of all file independent of disposition type. If it gets anything malicious even later, it sends a retrospective alert that contain complete history of threat.

Threat Containment

The Second step after the detection of threat and estimation of risk level is Threat Containment which involves the trace of threat. Any vulnerability to the network and devices within a network can result in information steel. Individual files and processes are traced in this step through Command and Control (C&C) Channels which help estimate trace of threat and spared of infection with in the network. The most important characteristic of this section is robust, extremely rapid and automatic threat containment process because the threat is to be disrupted along with the malicious activities started by the infection as soon as possible to prevent data loss.

Threat Containment can be followed through the following options:
1. Command and Control (C&C) Channels and Cognitive Threat Analytics (CTA) Integration.
2. Device and File trajectory.
3. Apply Policy to quarantine and Block communication.

Final Response and Remediation

The Last Responsive step which include remediation action techniques offers the clean-up for the environment. However, it is necessary to understand remediation action that the most rapid, immediate remediation action definitely secure the victim from imminent vulnerability of threat but it may could not remove malware completely. These threats contain several components and backup techniques to keep resisting. To prevent future attacks, determination of the root cause of these threat is necessary. Determination of root cause leads to the update of policy and threat intelligence which helps detection in the future.

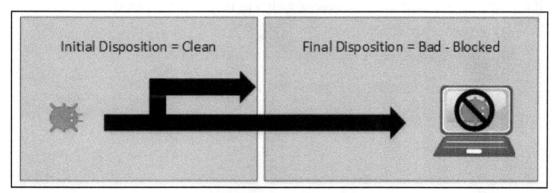

Figure 2-19: Retrospective Security

1. **Scanning for Additional Threats**

   Device trajectory, File trajectory and other tools can be run for re-inspection and continuous monitoring.

2. **Finding Root Cause**

   Root Cause analysis must be done. Root cause will help to close all ways to access.

3. **Clean up**

   Reimage, Endpoint cleaning tools can be used as require for clean-up.

4. **Policy update**

   Policies should have updated for future prevention.

Sandbox Analysis with Cisco AMP

Sandbox Technology

Sandboxing is one of the most important key component of network security. It supports security as an integrated component in a security solution. Cisco AMP Security Solution offers sandboxing which is much different from other traditional anti-virus and antimalware mechanisms. Cisco AMP Sandboxing technology offers enhanced protection by analysis of emerging threat in a sophisticated environment with in depth visibility and more granular control. Cisco AMP offers a focused infrastructure for sandboxing for dedicatedly analysing several hundred thousand of threats per day.

Sandboxing technology helps in detection of threat in a dedicated manner. During Sandboxing of a threat, Threat is searched in the Intelligence database for the analysis report. As Cisco AMP Sandboxing is capable to deal with large scale threats per day, it might be possible that diagnostics details are available if the threat is detected previously. When a threat is diagnosed before, its analytics are recorded for future use, it helps to diagnose now. If a match found is in the database, it helps in responding quickly.

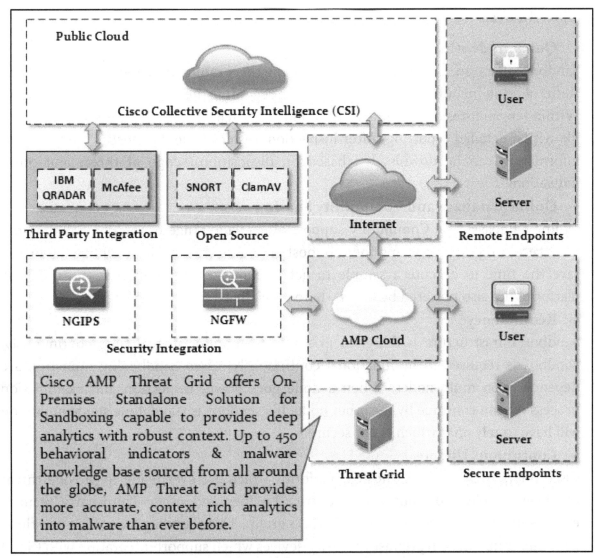

Cisco AMP Threat Grid offers On-Premises Standalone Solution for Sandboxing capable to provides deep analytics with robust context. Up to 450 behavioral indicators & malware knowledge base sourced from all around the globe, AMP Threat Grid provides more accurate, context rich analytics into malware than ever before.

Figure 2-20: Sandboxing with Cisco AMP

Sandboxing technology also provides protection when a file is uploading in the network. If file is known safe, it will be processed accordingly. In case the file is unknown, sandboxing offers an individual diagnostic operation. When the file is uploaded, it brings to the separate, sophisticated sandbox where it is inspected and analyzed with a fast and effective process. Final reports will lead to the action taken, however, results will be recorded in the database for future use.

Sandboxing within Cisco AMP Security Solution offers analysis of threats and malware using indicators. These indicators indicate regarding malicious activities and behaviour of the threat or suspicious file under diagnostics. Malicious behaviour is observed by Information theft, Behaviours of Applications, activities within the network, packet captures and other processes for observing the traffic.

Sandbox Analysis

- **Quick In-depth Analysis**

Sandbox offers an immediate response upon the examination request and provide status of result including detailed information regarding the sample under examination. Within few minutes of file upload, a sandbox can analyze and maintain records of the file with a detailed reporting. After inspection, result of the diagnostics, and detailed information can be downloaded based on disposition, scope of threat and other indications.

- **Online database and Community Sharing**

Online databases and Community support offers wide range of reports including the most recent reports regarding the top most emerging threat. These Online databased save the time to execute a sample to get intelligence report of that threat. These platforms are also powered by Cisco where officially reports are updated.

- **Redundancy**

Sandbox infrastructure is designed in a way to monitor in real time continuously. Sandbox is required to be functional continuously. Cisco Sandboxing infrastructure depends upon multi-nodes. When a node goes down, inspection and examination process remain continue by the other node. If a sandbox is standalone single node, you will have to rely on it which is not secure.

- **Continuous Update**

Cisco offers multiple cloud hosted platforms which are ever ready to provide threat intelligence collected from Cisco Security Engines and other Third-party security engines powered and monitored by TALOS group. This Cloud update offers real time, continuous update. On premises security devices which support integration with Cloud are being update continuously including Cisco AMP, AMP Threat Grid, Cisco ESA, Cisco WSA etc.

Sandbox Limitation

Sandboxing as defined offers its effective roles in Network Security deployment. However, Sandbox has some limitation that are still present after full integration deployment.

- In a sandboxing, when a certain malicious sample is under examination, there is not accuracy or guarantee that the malware is fully addressed along with its discreet components. There may be the possibility that the sample under diagnostic is not a complete malware, sandbox may be examining only a part of the malware. Other components of the malware may be waiting in several locations to be functional after assembling of all parts. In such a case, execution cannot be examined in a sandbox and it may only remove a part of malicious activity.

- Sandbox architecture is designed as alternate environment of real box used for analysing the malicious samples. Real box are the End user systems where malwares are actually executed. These sandboxes are not the as perfect the real box. Malicious threat might not function in sandbox as it functions on end user system, and vice versa.

- Malicious program executing in a sandbox might not have in depth information to classify as a threat. Similarly, malicious application can be similar to the legitimate one to be difficult to detect.

- These malicious program may set to be active after a certain period of time. This sleep mode will bring them out from sandbox and other scanning processes because no malicious behaviour will be observed as they are in sleep mode.

Cisco Advanced Malware Protection AMP Integration Options

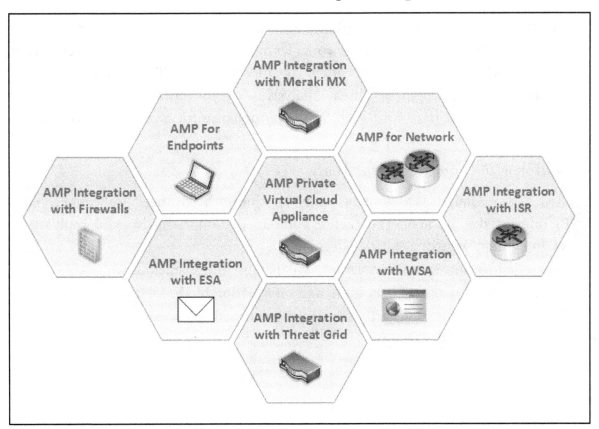

Figure 2-21: AMP Anywhere

Integration with Cloud Web Security (CWS)

Combined Solution of Cisco Advanced Malware Protection (AMP), Cloud Web Security (CWS) offers Malware protection and prevention from Public internet and infected User Endpoints infecting your corporate Network. It can also integrate with Cognitive Threat Analytics (CTA) and Web Security Appliance (WSA). These devices in combined integration offers more visibility, effective controlling and intelligence and defense from malwares.

Integration with Web Security Appliance (WSA)

Cisco Web Security Appliance in combination of Cisco Cloud Web Security (CWS), Cisco Advanced Malware Protection (AMP), offers next level advance protection against Web Security threats. This all-in-one High Level Web Security gateway provide the array of Web Security deployment features.

These advanced malwares and vulnerability even from secure site need an advanced web security solution which protect the network. To monitor the traffic and inspect filter the malicious traffic continuously, Cisco offers Advanced Malware Protection (AMP) offers protection of web with Cognitive Threat Analysis (CTA) for more enhanced security and performance to be integrate with Web Security Appliance for a complete Web Security Solution.

Integration with Cognitive Threat Analysis (CTA)

Cognitive Threat Analysis is a complementary solution with Advanced Malware Protection (AMP). Integrated Solution offers detection and remediation from advanced, sophisticated threats. Integrated Security Solution offers:

- Automatic Identification, Observation of malicious, and suspicious web data.
- Monitoring & validation of logs, alert, and information by the web security devices.
- Identification of anomalous activities based on normal behaviour.
- Device behaviour identification

AMP can be integrated with several other security engines.

Chapter 3: Cisco FirePOWER Next-Generation Intrusion Prevention System (NGIPS)

Introduction to Cisco FirePOWER NGIPS

Cisco FirePOWER offers Next-Generation Intrusion Prevention System, known as NGIPS, is one of the efficiently-proactive component in the Integrated Threat Security Solution. NGIPS provide stronger security layer with deep visibility, enhanced security intelligence and advanced protection against emerging threat in order to secure complex infrastructures of networks.

Cisco NGIPS Solution provide deep network visibility, automation, security intelligence, and next-level protection. It uses the most advanced and effective intrusion prevention capabilities to catch emerging sophisticated network attacks. It continuously collects information regarding network, including operating systems information, files and applications information, devices and user's information. This information helps NGIPS to determine network maps and host profiles which lead to contextual information to make better decisions about intrusive events.

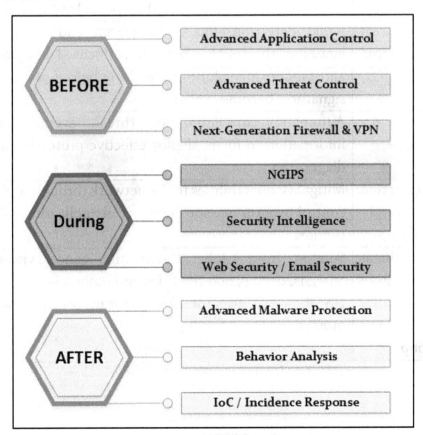

Figure 3-1: NGIPS Security

Using these information, Security Automation can also enable an efficient security feature offered by NGIPS. Using Security Automation, it helps by correlating the vulnerably and potential threat to the network with the intrusion. This correlation results in the focused analytics of the threat which is potentially more vulnerable to the network.

Cisco's Talos Security Intelligence and Research Group can also integrate with Cisco FirePOWER NGIPS in order to collect and update intelligence information. This intelligence information as defined previously, helps in correlation of emerging threats in real time, using the most powerful, largest scaled threat detection engine-based cloud. This information leads to the most precise and focused rules for Intrusion prevention.

Features & Benefits:

Features	Benefits
Superior effectiveness	Stop known and unknown threats on large scale using next-generation threat protection techniques. Immediate detection of Threats to reduce its impact and spread
Contextual awareness	With real-time in-depth visibility, enhanced control over the users, devices, applications, threats, and vulnerabilities.
Advanced threat protection and rapid remediation	Rapid detection, blocking, contain and remediation to emerging threats through Threat focused integrated AMP and sandboxing solutions. Patching before new software or signatures become available.
Security automation	Automatic correlation of threat events, contextual information to focus, deploy effective protection and boost diagnostics.
Granular application visibility and control	Mitigate vulnerabilities to the network through sophisticated control over up to 4000 commercial applications along with support.
Global threat intelligence from Cisco's Talos Security Intelligence and Research Group	Support from Global threat intelligence, visibility and analysis, over 35,000 IPS rules and embedded IP-, URL- and DNS-based security intelligence for up-to-the-minute threat protection

Table 3-01: Features of Cisco FirePOWER NGIPS

Configuring Cisco FirePOWER Next-Generation IPS NGIPS

Initial Setup Configuration

1. Log into the device from Console (Series 3 Device) with Monitor and Keyboard.

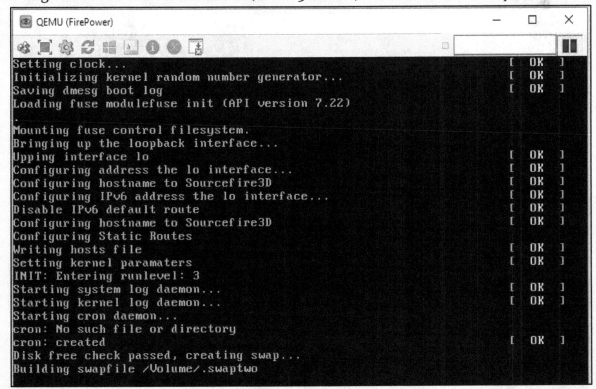

Figure 3-2: Sourcefire NGIPS booting process

2. Use "**admin**" as the username and "**Sourcefire**" as password. If computer is connected over Management interface use the address **192.168.45.45/24** to SSH to the default IPv4 address of Management Interface

3. Read and accept the EULA.

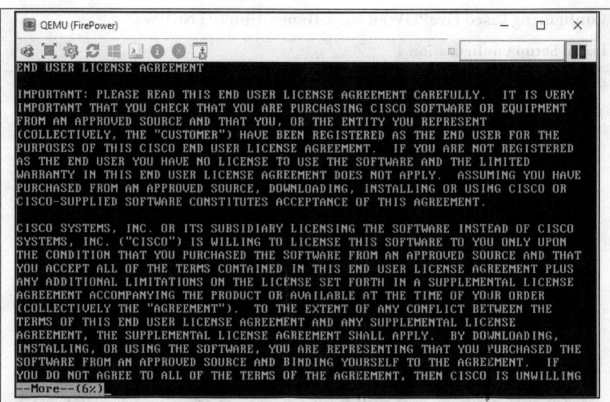

Figure 3-3: Sourcefire NGIPS EULA

4. Change the password for the admin account. This Administrator account has privileges and cannot be deleted. Login Credentials will remain same for accessing through CLI or GUI.

5. Configure network settings for the device.

   Configure (Enable or disable) IPv4 management settings

   Configure (Enable or disable) IPv6 management settings

   Configure IPv4 Dynamic or Manual settings

   Configure IPv6 addresses in colon-separated hexadecimal form.

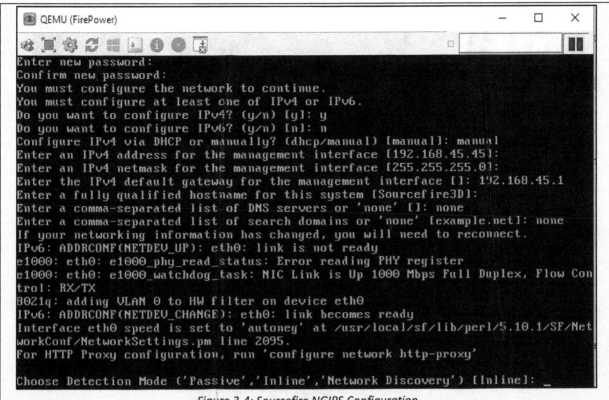

Figure 3-4: Sourcefire NGIPS Configuration

6. Select whether you want to allow changing of the device's network settings using the LCD panel.

7. Specify the detection mode based on how you deployed the device.

8. Issue the Command *Configure Manager add [hostname | ipv4 | ipv6 |DONTRESOLVE]*

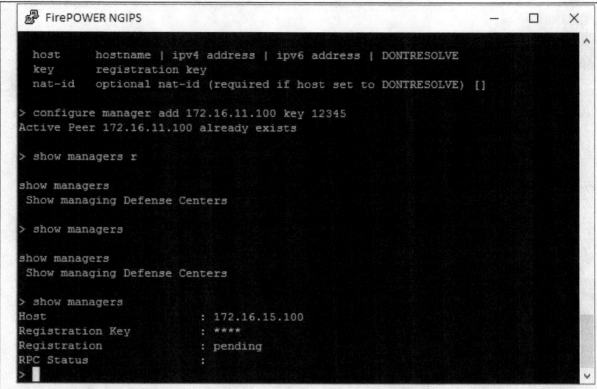

Figure 3-5

9. Now Login to FirePOWER Management Center Webpage to add Managed Device

Figure 3-6

10. Login and Navigate to *Devices > Device Management*

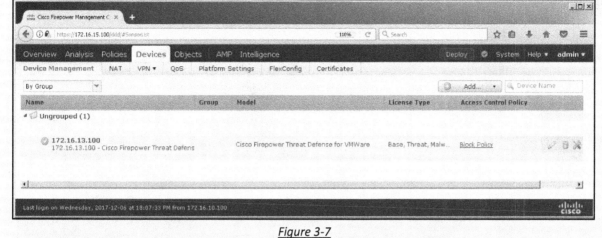

Figure 3-7

11. Click *Add* and Select *Add Device*

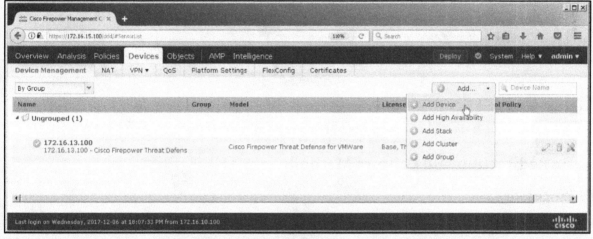

Figure 3-8

12. Configure the Host, Device Name, Registration key and other required attributes

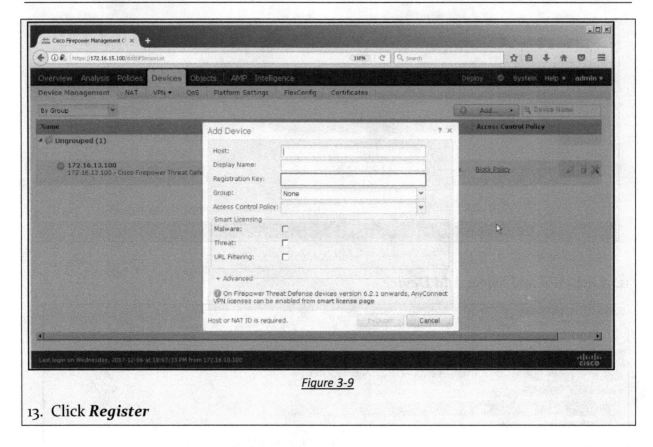

Figure 3-9

13. Click **Register**

Traffic Redirection and Capture Methods

Pre-Processors

There are three types of Pre-Processors used in NGIPS.

1. Application Layer Pre-processors
2. SCADA Pre-processors
3. Transport and Network Layer Pre-processors

Application Layer Pre-processors

Application Layer Pre-processors are designed especially for inspection of data running at the Application layer. Data running at the Application layer can be represented in different ways. However, the application layer processor is capable of decoding the traffic and diagnose the data type into the respective formats for examination. Examination and analytics of decoded data is with respect to the rules and policies configured on the Firepower device. Along with the decoding function by the Application Layer Pre-processors, it also performs normalizing encoding over the Application layer protocol which applies the rules on the packets.

Application layer Pre-processors are further classified into the following types:

- The DCE/RPC Pre-processor
- The DNS Pre-processor
- The FTP/Telnet Decoder
- The HTTP Inspect Pre-processor
- The Sun RPC Pre-processor
- The SIP Pre-processor
- The GTP Pre-processor
- The IMAP Pre-processor
- The POP Pre-processor
- The SMTP Pre-processor
- The SSH Pre-processor
- The SSL Pre-processor

1. DCE-RPC Pre-Processors

DCE / RPC Pre-processors ensure the multiple processes running on different host to communicate. This Inter-process communication used TCP and UDP Transport protocols. Using Transport Protocol TCP, DCE-RPC may further be encapsulated into Windows Server Message block (SMB). DCE-RPC protocol contain Unique headers. TCP header is 24-bytes and UDP header is 80-bytes.

Enabling the DCE/RPC pre-processor will automatically enable default target-based policy. Additionally, other target-based policies can also be added that target other hosts running different Windows or Samba versions. The default target-based policy applies to any host not included in another target-based policy.

These DCE/RPC option offers the configuration to set the controlling of the processor. Any Option except Memory-Cap, Auto-Detect and SMB inspection may degrade the performance of the device.

- Maximum Fragment Size
- Reassembly Threshold
- Enable Defragmentation
- Memory Cap Reached
- Auto-Detect policy on SMB Session
- Legacy SMB Inspection Mode

2. DNS Pre-Processors

DNS Pre-Processor examine the Domain Name Server responses. This DNS Server Response is based on three components including on a Message Header, Query, Response with detailed information. DNS Reponses provide the IP address, or addresses resolved by the DNS including name server information that resolve the query.

3. ***FTP and Telnet Decoder***

The FTP/Telnet decoder analyzes FTP and telnet data by performing Stateful or Stateless inspection. It normalizes FTP and telnet commands before processing by the rules engine.

4. ***HTTP Inspect Pre-Processor***

HTTP Inspect Pre-Processor decodes and normalize HTTP request that are sent and received from the web servers because HTTP traffic can be encoded in different formats to make it complex but HTTP inspect encoder is capable to decode up to 14 formats of encoding. It also segregates the packets received URL, Cookie and Non-Cookie Headers and Body. This segregation into components improves the performance by detecting URL encoding threats.

5. **Sun RPC Pre-Processor**

The Sun RPC (Remote Procedure Call) Pre-Processor normalize the RPC records into a single record. RPC records are generated into fragments which are unified in a record for the evaluation according to the rules.

RPC pre-processor options include:

- Ports
- Detection of fragmented RPC records
- Detect multiple records in one packet
- Detect single fragment records with respect to size of a packet
- Detect fragmented record sums which exceed one fragment

6. ***SIP Pre-Processor***

SIP (Session Initiation Protocol) provides services to application like Instant messaging, Online gaming, Internet telephony etc. SIP protocol contains information regarding the purpose of request, destination URL, status codes, and etc. SIP uses Real-time Transport protocol for communication. SIP Pre-Processor is responsible for decoding of SIP traffic and analyze the traffic. It segregates SIP header, body of the message and other components and compare against the configured rule for inspection.

7. ***GTP Pre-Processor***

General Service Packet Radio (GPRS) Tunnelling Protocol is termed as GTP, provides communication over a GTP core network. The GTP Pre-Processor is used to detects anomalies in GTP network traffic and send command channel signalling messages to the rules engine for inspection.

8. ***POP Pre-Processor***

The Post Office Protocol (POP) is used for the Email communication between Client and POP Server. The POP pre-processor inspects this communication i.e. server-to-

client POP3 traffic. If pre-processor rules are enabled, it generates events on anomalous traffic. It can also extract and decode email attachments.

9. *SMTP Pre-Processor*

The SMTP pre-processor normalize the SMTP commands along with extracting and decoding email attachments in client-to-server traffic. Some software versions can extract other details like file name, address, and header data. Normalization can be enabled and disabled.

10. *SSH Pre-Processor*

SSH Pre-Processor offer the detection of the following
- The Challenge-Response Buffer Overflow exploit
- The CRC-32 exploit
- The SecureCRT SSH Client Buffer Overflow exploit
- Protocol mismatches
- Incorrect SSH message direction
- Any version string other than version 1 or 2

11. *SSL Pre-Processor*

SSL Pre-Processor offer SSL inspection offering blocking capability of encrypted traffic, decrypting and diagnostics of encrypted traffic along with access control. SSL Pre-processor does not require a license for decrypting the traffic however other services by SSL Pre-Processor requires a protection license.

SCADA Pre-processors

Supervisory control and data acquisition (SCADA) is a control protocol that uses computers, networked data communications and graphical user interfaces for high-level process supervisory management, monitoring and controlling and acquiring of data. Cisco FirePOWER offers SCADA pre-Processors for Modbus and DNP3 SCADA protocols.

1. *Modbus Pre-Processor*

The Modbus pre-processor detects anomalies in Modbus traffic. Modbus pre-processor decodes the Modbus protocol and proceed for processing by the rules engine. There are some Modbus pre-processor rules which must be enabled to generate events.

Modbus Pre-Processor Rule	Description
144:1	To generate event, when length of Modbus header does not match the length required by the Modbus function code.
144:2	To generate an event when the Modbus protocol ID is non-zero
144:3	To generate an event when the pre-processor detects a reserved Modbus function code.

Table 3-02: Modbus Pre-Processor Rules

2. DNP3 Pre-Processor

The DNP3 pre-processor is used to detect anomalies in DNP3 traffic. It decodes the DNP3 protocol for processing by rules engine. Following are the DNP rules list and description which are enabled to generate desired alerts for the events.

DNP3 Pre-Processor Rule	Description
145:1	For generating an event when it detects a link layer frame with an invalid checksum.
145:2	Generates an event and blocks the packet when it detects a DNP3 link layer frame with an invalid length.
145:3	Generates an event and blocks the packet during reassembly it detects a transport layer segment with an invalid sequence number.
145:4	Generates an event when the DNP3 reassembly buffer is cleared before a complete fragment can be reassembled. This happens when a segment carrying the FIR flag appears after other segments have been queued.
145:5	Generates an event when the pre-processor detects a DNP3 link layer frame that uses a reserved address.
145:6	Generates an event when the pre-processor detects a DNP3 request or response that uses a reserved function code.

Table 17: DNP3 Pre-Processor Rules

Transport & Network Layer Pre-processors

Transport and Network Layer Pre-processors are used to detect threats using IP fragmentation pre-processor, Checksum validation, TCP and UDP session pre-processing. Before the packet processed by the Transport and Network Layer Pre-processors, packet is sent to decoders which decode and segregate the Packet header and body into format to be easily handled by pre-processors. Transport and Network Layer Pre-processors. If rule engine is configured for an intrusion rule which requires a disabled pre-processor, it will automatically get its services even remaining it disabled on network analysis policy's web interface.

Major process in Transport and Network Layer Pre-Processing includes
- Checksum Verification
- The Inline Normalization Pre-processor
- The IP Defragmentation Pre-processor
- The Packet Decoder
- TCP Stream Pre-processing
- UDP Stream Pre-processing

1. Checksum Verification

Checksum verification process includes checksum calculation at protocol level to ensure the tampering of packets send and receiving throughout the network. Protocol which are evaluated for checksum are IP, TCP UDP and ICMP protocols. Checksum verification process also verify the integrity of the Protocol of packet using an algorithm. Network is considered as susceptible or unsecure if Checksum verification is disabled however it does not guarantee the verification event.

Checksum Verification Options
- ICMP Checksum
- IP Checksum
- TCP Checksum
- UDP Checksum

2. The Inline Normalization Pre-processor

Inline Normalization Pre-Processor provide normalization of traffic in order to reduce the vulnerability of evading by the process of detection in inline mode. Inline Normalization process is conducted just after decoder. After Inline Normalization, Packet is forwarded to other processors. Normally, Inline Normalization Pre-Processor handle the Normalization on per-packet basis. IPv4, IPv6, ICMPv4, ICMPv6 and TCP packets can be configured to be normalized. Inline Normalization Pre-Processor is not capable to generate events, it only processes the packets to make them ready to be use by other processors and rule engine.

Inline Normalization Options

Option	Description
Normalize ICMPv4	Normalization of ICMPv4 clears the 8-bit code in echo request and echo reply in ICMPv4 Traffic.
Normalize ICMPv6	Normalization of ICMPv6 clears the 8-bit code in echo request and echo reply in ICMPv6 Traffic.
Normalize/clear reserved bit	Normalize/clear reserved bit in TCP Header

Normalize/clear option padding bytes	Normalize/clear option padding bytes clears any TCP option padding bytes.
Clear urgent pointer	Clears the 16-bit TCP header Urgent Pointer field if the urgent (URG) control bit is not set.
Clear Urgent Pointer/URG on empty payload	Clears the TCP header Urgent Pointer field and the URG control bit if there is no payload.
Normalize urgent pointer	Sets the two-byte TCP header Urgent Pointer field to the payload length if the pointer is greater than the payload length.
Remove Data on Syn	Removes data in synchronization (SYN) packets if your TCP operating system policy is not Mac OS.
Trim Data to MSS	Trims the TCP Data field to the size specified in the Window field.
Block Unrecoverable TCP header anomalies	Trims the TCP Data field to the Maximum Segment Size (MSS) if the payload is longer than MSS.
Normalize/clear option padding bytes	Blocking of Unrecoverable TCP header anomalies means blocking TCP packets if when normalized becomes invalid.

Table 3-03: Inline Normalization Options

3. The IP Defragmentation Pre-processor

IP fragmentation process is based on breaking down IP datagram into smaller datagrams because of limitation of Maximum Transfer Unit (MTU). IP defragmentation process is based on re-assembling of fragmented IP datagrams into the original IP datagram which is traditionally re-assembled at receiving side.

A datagram may be containing a threat along with it which may not be identified because of fragmentation of IP datagram as a part of threat may lie in a fragmented IP datagram, similarly other may lie in other fragmented datagrams. It can re-assemble at the destination and start propagating within the network. IP defragmentation Pre-Processor offers reassembling of fragmented IP datagrams so that the fragmented datagrams can be combined to inspect. If defragmentation could not successfully reassemble any stream of packets, Rule engine cannot execute it process over them.

4. The Packet Decoder

When a datagram is verified by its checksum, before forwarding the captured packets to a pre-processors and rules engine for processing, these packets are first pass through the packet decoder. The packet decoder segregate packet's headers and payloads into a format. This formatting helps pre-processors and the rules engine to process these

packets with ease. Each stack layer is decoded, Starting from data link, through the network and transport layers.

Packet Decoder Option includes

➢ Decoding of Encapsulated GTP (General Packet Radio Service (GPRS) Tunnelling

➢ Protocol) Data Channel

➢ Detection of Teredo Tunnelling of IPv6 on Non-Standard Port (other than UDP port 3544)

➢ Detection of Excessive Length Value (Detection of Header length and Actual length mismatch)

➢ Detect Invalid IP Option

➢ Detection of Experimental TCP Options

➢ Detection of Obsolete TCP Option

➢ Detection of Other TCP options

Option	Option Type	Description
9	Experimental	Partial Order Connection Permitted
10	Experimental	Partial Order Service Profile
14	Experimental	Alternate Checksum Request
15	Experimental	Alternate Checksum Data
18	Experimental	Trailer Checksum
20	Experimental	Space Communications Protocol Standards (SCPS)
21	Experimental	Selective Negative Acknowledgements (SCPS)
22	Experimental	Record Boundaries (SCPS)
23	Experimental	Corruption (SPCS)
24	Experimental	SNAP
26	Experimental	TCP Compression Filter
6	Obsolete	Echo
7	Obsolete	Echo Reply
16	Obsolete	Skeeter
17	Obsolete	Bubba
19	Obsolete	MD5 Signature
25	Obsolete	Unassigned

Table 3-04: Decoder Options

5. TCP Stream Pre-processing

TCP transport protocol can classify the connection state by identifying a TCP connection by the address and Ports. Addresses may include Source and destination addresses and port are comprised of Source and Destination ports. TCP Stream Pre-Processor may also inspect for the traffic which is not identified as TCP Session but it's not a recommended technique. TCP only allows a connection with same parameter. For explaining it in even better way, consider an example of a corporate network attacked by Stick or Snot. These attacks create and flow the packets containing snort intrusion rules throughout the network. If the Stateful inspection is not configured by using flow or flowbits' keywords, these rouge packets can trigger the rule. In the other hand, if Stateful inspection is configured these packets will be ignored as they are not part of Established TCP session.

6. UDP Stream Pre-Processing

UDP stream Pre-processing can be enabled by configuring the rule engine with the UDP rule containing flow keyword with any argument like Established, To client, From Client, To Server, or from Server. As we know UDP is connectionless protocol. UDP stream Pre-Processor evaluate the direction and session of UDP traffic by its Source and Destination IP address, Header and ports. UDP Stream Pre-Processing may have configured to close the stream after specified number of time (in sec) inactivity and delete the entry form state table. Additionally, Pre-Processor can also ignore and discard the UDP traffic on all ports and applications according to the configured rule.

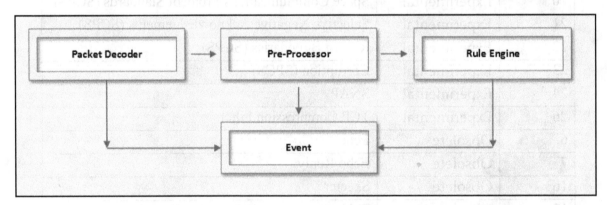

Figure 3-10: Transport & Network Layer Pre-Processing Flow

Detection Engines

There are number of pre-processors which can be used in a policy in order to detect particular threats vulnerable to the network, such as Back Orifice, port scan, and Rate-based attacks. These attacks may attempt to overwhelm the network with excessive traffic. As defined, when any intrusion rule required for a disabled pre-processor, the system will automatically use it with the current configuration. Regardless, it remains disabled in the network analysis policy's web interface.

Black Orifice Detection

Back Orifice is a program which can make a system completely administered by a remote user (attacker). It allows the hacker to get the files and is capable to modify them. The FirePOWER offers the Back Orifice Detection Pre-Processor which is capable to detect the existence of back orifice program. The Back Orifice pre-processor examines UDP traffic against the Back Orifice magic cookie i.e. "*!*QWTY?". This magic cookie is located in the first eight bytes of the packet and is XOR-encrypted.

Port Scan Detection

Port Scanning is the examination procedure that is mostly used by the attackers to identify the open port. However, it may also be used by the legitimate users. Port scanning is does not always lead to an attack as it used by both of them,. However, it is a network reconnaissance that can be used before an attack to collect information. In this scenario, special packets are forwarded to a particular host, whose response are examined by the attacker to get information regarding open ports. FirePOWER offers PortScan Detector that is designed for this purpose to monitor the ports scanning that may lead to malicious activity.

Port Scan detector inspect the port scanning processes by observing the negative responses from the host that generate probes. When the Detector detects a negative response, it records the response. Port scan detector will generate the event based on the sensitivity level. Sensitivity levels are:

- Low
- Medium
- High

Type	Description
PortScan Detection	A one-to-one PortScan, an attacker against one or a few hosts to scan on or multiple ports. PortScan are characterized by: • Low number of scanning hosts • Single host that is scanned • High number of ports scanned This option detects TCP, UDP, and IP PortScan.
Port Sweep	A one-to-many port sweep, an attacker against one or a few hosts to scan a single port on multiple target hosts. Port sweeps are characterized by: • Low number of scanning hosts • High number of scanned hosts • Low number of unique ports scanned This option detects TCP, UDP, ICMP, and IP port sweeps.
Decoy PortScan	A one-to-one PortScan, attacker mixes spoofed source IP addresses with the actual scanning IP address. Decoy PortScan are characterized by: • High number of scanning hosts • Low number of ports that are scanned only once • Single or low number of scanned hosts The decoy PortScan option detects TCP, UDP, and IP protocol PortScan.
Distributed PortScan	A many-to-one PortScan in which multiple hosts query a single host for open ports. Distributed PortScan are characterized by: • High number of scanning hosts • High number of ports that are scanned only once • Single or low number of scanned hosts The distributed PortScan option detects TCP, UDP, and IP protocol PortScan.

Table 3-05: Port Scan Type

Rate-Based Attack Prevention

Rate-based attack prevention is the prevention against the attacks that depend upon the frequency or number of repetition of connection attempts to attack. Rate-based detection is used to detect a rate-based attack. Configuring the policy to include the inspection of rate-based attacks using rate-based filters that filters the excessive activity. SYN attack prevention protect against SYN floods, by protecting hosts and network from the ratio of Number of packet over period of time.

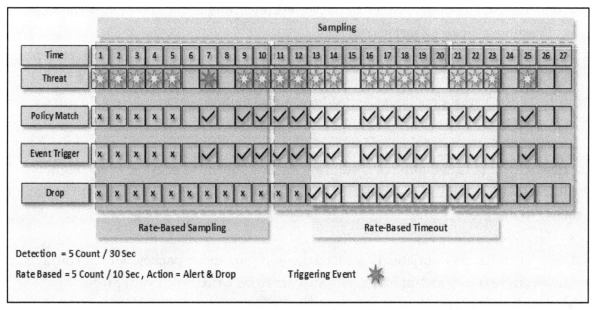

Figure 3-11: Rate-Based Sampling

In the figure above, Rate-based detection is configured as 5 Count within 30 seconds, rate-based detection is configured for 5 counts within 10 seconds and timeout interval of 10 seconds. Continuous 5 Count from time interval 1 to 5 gets ready for triggering the event. 6th Count trigger the event as its fulfil the condition of 5 Count within 30 seconds and only event is triggered without dropping packets. After triggering the event, Rate-based Count starts which gets 5 Count with 10 Seconds in between 7th Sec till 12th Second. As the Condition fulfils, it starts Event and Drop action for 10 Seconds (i.e. Rate-based Timeout).

Event Actions and Suppression Thresholds

Event Actions are the actions that are taken by the FirePOWER device when an event is triggered. These actions includes generation of alerts, initiation of logging, Blocking and denial of Packet, Connection, and generating requests. Configuring or modification an Event Action list requires a new list for event action which will replace the old event action list.

Alert and Log Actions

Alert and Log action offers generation of alert when an event is triggered along with logging to have a trace to the activity. There are different alerts option available in alert and logging action which are as follows.

- **Produce Alert**

Produce Alert record, or write the event when it triggers in the Event store as an alert. Produce Alert has to be enabled to have alert regarding event added in event store.

- **Produce Verbose Alert**

Produce Verbose alert is the option which is an encoded dump of the detected packet in the alert. This collection of encoded dump action generates an alert to the Event Store. It can alert independent of Produce Alert i.e. it can generate alert if Produce alert is not enabled.

- **Log Attacker Packets**

Log Attacker packets initiates IP address logging for those packets which contains the attacker address and sends an alert. This action causes an alert (independent of Produce alert) to the Event Store.

- **Log Victim Packets**

Log Victim Packets initiates IP address Logging for those packets which contains the victim address. Log victim also sends an alert to be written to Event Store.

- **Log Pair Packets**

Log Pair Packets initiates IP Logging for the packets containing the attacker and victim address pair. This action causes an alert (independent of Produce alert) to the Event Store.

- **Request SNMP Trap**

Request SNMP Trap requests the Notification Application component of the sensor; the sensor must be configured with SNMP. These requests are to perform SNMP notification. This action causes an alert (independent of Produce alert) to the Event Store.

Deny Actions

- **Deny Packet Inline**

Deny packet inline action ensures the termination of the packet in the inline mode.

- **Deny Connection Inline**

Deny connection inline action ensures the termination of current and the upcoming packets on this TCP flow.

- **Deny Attacker-Victim-Pair Inline**

Deny Attacker-Victim-Pair inline action does not transmit the captured packet and upcoming packets containing the attacker/victim address pair for a specified period of time.

- ***Deny Attacker Service Pair Inline***

Deny Attacker Service Pair Inline action does not transmit the captured packets and the upcoming packets containing the attacker address victim port pair for a specified period of time.

- ***Deny Attacker Inline***

Deny Attacker Inline action terminates the current packet and upcoming packets from this attacker address for a specified period of time. The sensor records the list of attackers, that are being denied by the system.

- ***Modify Packet Inline***

Modify Packet Inline action modifies the data of the captured packets to remove suspicious, malicious components and ambiguity about what the end point might do with the packet.

Other Actions

- ***Request Block Connection***

Request block connection action forwards a request to ARC to block this connection. Request-block-connection requires a blocking devices configured to enforce this action.

- ***Request Block Host***

Request block host action forwards a request to ARC to block the host (attacker). Request block host action requires a blocking devices configured to enforce this action.

- **Request Rate Limit**

Request rate limit action forwards a request to ARC to perform rate limiting. Request rate limit action requires a rate limiting device configured to enforce this action.

- **Reset TCP Connection**

Reset TCP Connection action forwards TCP reset requests to terminate the TCP flow. Reset TCP Connection requires TCP signatures to analyze a single connection. It does not work for sweeps or floods.

Event Suppression and Threshold

Suppression and Threshold offers the capability to minimize the event alerts for the same event generating by the number of detection triggering again and again. Using threshold and suppression techniques, event notification can be limit. Threshold support individual rule or per policy configuration. Threshold offers the limitation of system logs and alert an event depending upon number of time event is triggered with respect to time. Suppression of an intrusion event notification is capable of detecting and suppressing the event notification from the specified IP address or the range of IP address triggering the events.

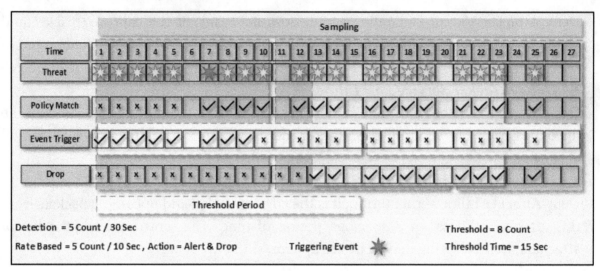

Figure 3-12: Threshold Period

Correlation Policies

Using the Correlation Policy feature provides capability to respond to the threat propagating in your network in real time. Correlation Policy correlates and monitor the activities against the Correlation Policy rules, and search for policy violation i.e. any activity triggering the rule or compliance with whitelist associated with an active correlation policy.

Correlation Rules

Correlation policy is based upon the configured correlation rules. These rules are the reason for generation of correlation event. Correlation rules are associated with the conditions which can trigger a correlation rule includes the system generating events like connection event, intrusion event, malware detection, discovery, user activity, and more. Correlation rule can also trigger when network traffic deviates from its normal profile.

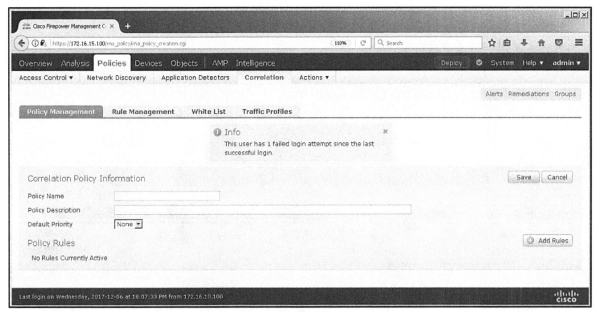

Figure 3-13

Additional Configuration parameters to contain correlation rules includes

Additional Parameters	Description
Host Profile Qualification	Use Host Profile Information in correlation of the host, involved in the triggering event
Connection Tracker	If Certain condition matches, System initiates tracking the connection
User Qualification	Tracking against the involvement of certain user or group of user
Snooze Periods	When an event is triggered, Snooze period prevent it to trigger again for specified interval.
Inactive Periods	Correlation rule will not trigger for inactive period.

Table 3-06: Correlation Policy Constrains

Compliance Whitelist

Compliance White list is the list which specifies operating systems, Web applications, Client applications, and protocols. These configured OS, Application and protocol of Whitelist are allowed on host side within a network. In case, if a host violates white list, associated with an active correlation policy, the system generates a white list event.

Configuring Correlation Policies

1. Choose **Policies** > **Correlation**.
2. Click **Create Policy**.
3. Enter a Policy Name and Policy Description.
4. From the Default Priority drop-down list, choose a priority for the policy. Choose None to use rule priorities only.

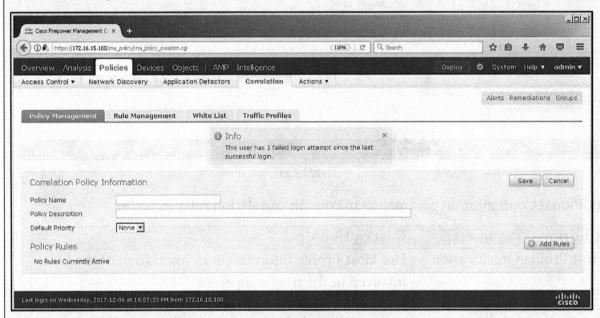

Figure 3-14

5. Click **Add Rules**, check the rules and white lists that you want to use in the policy, then click Add.

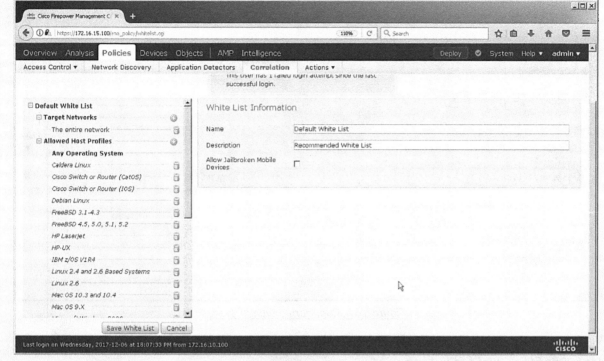

Figure 3-15

6. From the Priority list for each rule or white list, choose a priority:

    A) A priority value from 1 to 5

    B) None

    C) Default to use the policy's default priority

7. Add responses to rules and white lists

8. Click **Save**.

Configuring Correlation Rules

1. Choose **Policies > Correlation**, then click the **Rule Management** tab.

2. Click **Create Rule**.

3. Enter a Rule Name and Rule Description.

4. Optionally, choose a Rule Group for the rule.

5. Choose a base event type and, optionally, specify additional trigger criteria for the correlation rule. You can choose the following base event types:

```
Intrusion event occurs- [Syntax for Intrusion Event Trigger Criteria]
Malware event occurs- [Syntax for malware event Trigger Criteria]
Discovery event occurs- [Syntax for discovery Event Trigger Criteria]
User activity event occurs- [Syntax for user activity Trigger Criteria]
Host input event occurs- [Syntax for host input Event Trigger Criteria]
Connection event occurs- [Syntax for Connection Event Trigger Criteria]
Traffic profile event occurs- [Syntax for traffic profile Event Trigger
Criteria]
```

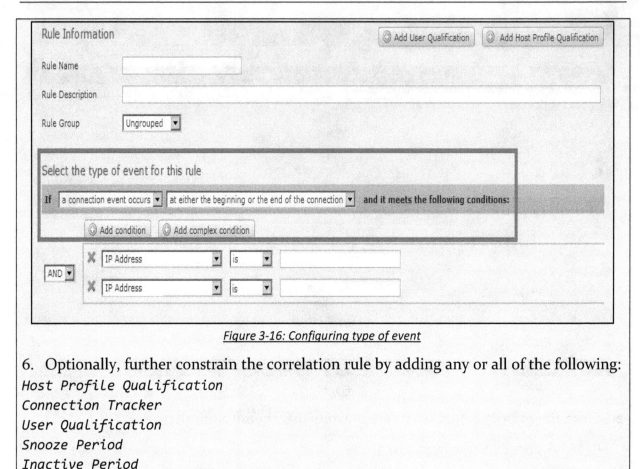

Figure 3-16: Configuring type of event

6. Optionally, further constrain the correlation rule by adding any or all of the following:

Host Profile Qualification
Connection Tracker
User Qualification
Snooze Period
Inactive Period

7. Click **Save Rule.**

SNORT Rules

SNORT

Snort is an open source intrusion prevention system offered by Cisco which delivers the most effective and comprehensive real-time network defense solutions. Snort is capable of protocol analysis, real-time packet analysis and logging. It can also search and filter content, detect a wide variety of attacks and probes including buffer overflows, port scans, SMB probes and much more. Snort can also be used in various forms including packet sniffer, a packet logger, network file logging device, or as a full-blown network intrusion prevention system.

Snort Rule

Rules are a criterion for performing detection against threats and vulnerabilities to the system and network, which leads to the advantage of zero-day detection. Unlike signatures, rules are focused on detecting the actual vulnerabilities. There are two ways to get Snort rules:

1. Snort Subscribers Rule
2. Snort Community Rule

There is no much difference in between Snort Subscribers rule and Community rule. However, Subscriber rules are updated frequently and updated on the device as well. It requires a paid subscription to get real time updates of Snort Rules. Community rules are updated by Snort Community containing all rules as the Subscribers set of rule contains but they are not updated quickly as subscriber rule are.

Categories of Snort Rules

Snort rules are categorized in different categories and updated frequently by TALOS. Some of these categories are

Application Detection Rule Category that includes the rules monitoring, Controlling of traffic of certain application. These rules control the behaviour and network activities of these applications.

- app-detect.rules

Black List Rules category include the URL, IP address, DNS and other rules that have been determined to be indicator of malicious activities.

- blacklist.rules

Browsers Category include the rule for detection of vulnerabilities in certain browsers.

- browser-chrome.rules
- browser-firefox.rules
- browser-ie.rules
- browser-webkit
- browser-other
- browser-plugins

Operating System Rules category include rules looking for vulnerabilities in OS

- os-solaris
- os-windows
- os-mobile
- os-linux
- os-other

Similarly, there are number of categories and types of rules.

SSL Decryption Policy

Overview

SSL Policy is FirePOWER devices is used to control dealing with encrypted traffic within the network. These SSL Policies handle the encrypted traffic using configured action. These actions are enforced over encrypted and non-encrypted traffic. SSL policies are associated with the Access Control Policies that deal with the incoming packets by decrypting the encrypted packets.

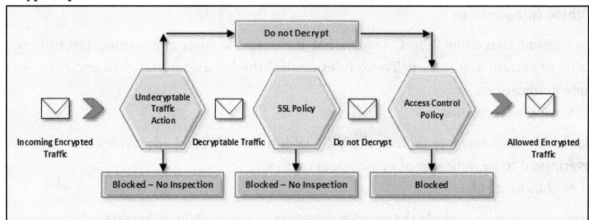

Figure 3-17: SSL Policy flow

Deployment and removal of SSL policies interrupt the inspection temporarily. It may block and pass the packets without inspection in this interval. SSL Policy basic flow directs the device to handle the encrypted packets with a default action. This default action may configure to block Undecryptable packets or to allow for further inspection by the access control policy.

Default Handling Options for Undecryptable Traffic

Type	Default Action	Available Options
SSLv2 Session	Inherit Default action	Do not decrypt Block Block with reset Inherit default action
Unknown Cipher	Inherit Default action	Do not decrypt Block Block with reset Inherit default action
Non-Supported Cipher	Inherit Default action	Do not decrypt Block Block with reset Inherit default action
Session not cached	Inherit Default action	Do not decrypt Block

		Block with reset
		Inherit default action
Handshaking Errors	Inherit Default action	Do not decrypt
		Block
		Block with reset
		Inherit default action
Decryption Errors	Block	Block
		Block with reset

Table 3- 07: Default handling Options

Configuring Basic SSL Policy

1. Choose **Policies** > **Access Control** > **SSL.**
2. Click **New Policy**.
3. Give the policy a unique Name and, optionally, a Description.
4. Specify the Default Action
5. Configure logging options for the default action.
6. Click Save.

Default Action	Enforcement of Encrypted Packets
Block	Block SSL session without inspection
Block with Reset	Block SSL session without inspection and Reset TCP Connection
Do not Decrypt	Inspect Encrypted packets with Access Control Policy

Table 3-08: SSL Default Policy Actions

Cisco FirePOWER NGIPS Deployment

Deployment Modes

Cisco FirePOWER device can be deployed using any of the two modes. Inline Mode Deployment or Passive mode can have deployed. There is some difference in these Modes such as Out-of-band or transparent flow which can be adopted as required.

Passive Mode Deployment

In a passive mode of deployment, the Firepower device monitors the incoming and outgoing traffic flowing through the network with the help of a Switch Port Analyzer (SPAN) or by using mirror port. In the passive mode, system deployment is out of band from the traffic. The Switch Port Analyzer (SPAN) or mirror port make copies of traffic flowing from other ports on the switch. Passive interfaces receive the traffic, unconditionally and nothing received on these interfaces is retransmitted. Passive interface may include Outbound traffic containing flow control packets.

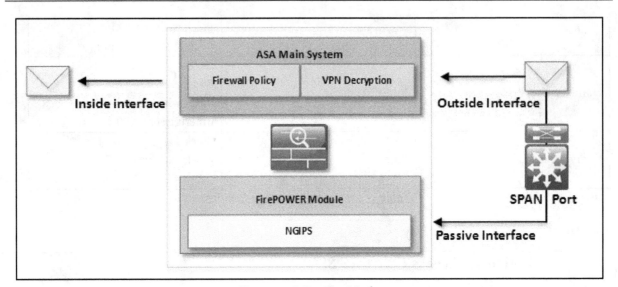

Figure 3-18: Passive Mode

This duplication provides visibility for monitoring and granular control across the network without effecting the traffic flow. In Passive Mode Deployment, some feature is limited like system cannot take actions such as blocking or shaping of traffic.

Inline Mode Deployment

Inline FirePOWER NGIPS deployment offers transparent configuration of Firepower System by binding two ports together. This binding allows the FirePOWER system to be compatible in any network architecture without requiring the adjacent network devices. Inline interfaces receive the traffic unconditionally as in passive mode, but this received unconditional traffic on these interfaces are retransmitted out of an inline set unless explicitly dropped.

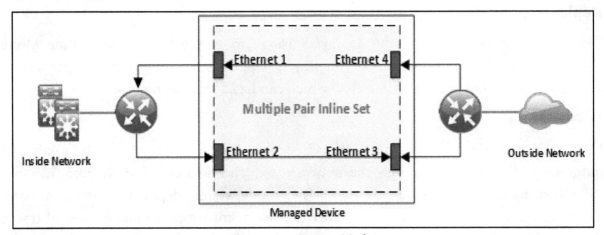

Figure 3-19: Passive Mode

Inline Interface pair

In the Inline Mode deployment, Inline interfaces configuration is required before use. Inline sets are to be configured which contains interface pairs. Basically, Inline sets are the group that contains one pair of inline interfaces or more. An inline interface pair can associate with an inline set at a time. Configuration of Inline Set include:

Configuration Parameters	Details
Name	Name for Inline Set
interfaces	Associated Inline interface Pairs
MTU	MTU for Inline Set
Failsafe	Allow traffic to bypass detection and continue
Bypass Mode	Bypass mode when interfaces fails (FirePOWER 7000 and 8000 Series only)

Table 3-09: Inline Set Configuration Options

Inline Tap Mode

Line Tap Mode option is offered by Cisco FirePOWER 7000 and 8000 Series. Inline Tap Mode is associated with inline or Inline with Fail-open interface sets. Tap mode feature in inline deployment requires only a copy of network traffic flowing instead of the original traffic flow through the device. In this way, Traffic flowing across the network remain undisturbed as it deals with the copies of packets. Rule and policies configured in inline tap mode does not affect the packet stream but they do generate the alert and events of intrusive events. The table shows the events indicating triggering packets that would have dropped in inline deployment.

The main advantage of Inline Tap mode is for the network testing or troubleshooting scenario in which capturing of various type of intrusion events can be monitored that which packets are triggering the intrusion event and examination of policy actions to take certain action to modify the policies if it is not working efficiently. Later on, inline tap mode can be disabled and shift the deployment to Inline mode.

Cisco FirePOWER NGIPS Deployment

Cisco FirePOWER NGIPS Module with ASA

The Adaptive Security Appliance (ASA) with FirePOWER module delivers Next-Generation Intrusion Prevention System (NGIPS), including next-generation firewall services, Application Visibility and Control (AVC), URL filtering, and Advanced Malware Protection (AMP). ASA with FirePOWER module uses an application from the ASA. This module can be either hardware module or a software module. Separate hardware module is offer for ASA 5585-X only whereas software module is introduced for all other models. ASA FirePOWER module can be deployed using the following Deployment models

1. Inline Mode
2. Inline Tap Monitor-only Mode
3. Passive Monitor-Only Mode

```
ASA                                                    —    □    ×

System initialization in progress. Please stand by. You must change the password
 for 'admin' to continue. Enter new password: <new password>
Confirm new password: <repeat password>
You must configure the network to continue.
You must configure at least one of IPv4 or IPv6.
Do you want to configure IPv4? (y/n) [y]: y
Do you want to configure IPv6? (y/n) [n]:
Configure IPv4 via DHCP or manually? (dhcp/manual) [manual]:
Enter an IPv4 address for the management interface [192.168.45.45]:198.51.100.3
Enter an IPv4 netmask for the management interface [255.255.255.0]: 255.255.255.0
Enter the IPv4 default gateway for the management interface []: 198.51.100.1
Enter a fully qualified hostname for this system [Sourcefire3D]: asasfr.example.com
Enter a comma-separated list of DNS servers or 'none' []:
198.51.100.15, 198.51.100.14 Enter a comma-separated list of search domains or 'none'
[example.net]: example.com If your networking information has changed, you will need to
reconnect. For HTTP Proxy configuration, run 'configure network http-proxy
```

Figure 3-20 : NGIPS Deployment

ASA FirePOWER Management

ASA FirePOWER module has Command line interface (CLI). Command Line Interface can perform initial configuration and troubleshooting. In order to configure Security Policies on ASA FirePOWER module, following methods can utilize:

- **Firepower/FireSIGHT Management Center**

Firepower/FireSIGHT Management Center offers deployment option including hosted on separate Management Center appliance as well as a virtual appliance. The Management Centre application is named "FireSIGHT". In version 6.0, called FirePOWER.

- **ASDM**

ASDM also offers the manageability for FirePOWER module for the devices having compatible model and versions.

Both, Firepower/FireSIGHT Management Center and ASDM cannot be used. Any one option has to be deployed for Management.

ASA Features Compatibility with FirePOWER Module

- Although ASA offers advanced features and services such as Advanced HTTP inspection but using with FirePOWER module provide even Next-level inspection for HTTP as compared to ASA. Using ASA with FirePOWER module for HTTP inspection are not compatible with each other, Recommended configuration to prevent compatibility issues is not to configure ASA HTTP inspection over the traffic directed to FirePOWER module.
- Mobile User Security (MUS) server is not even compatible with Cisco ASA FirePOWER module, do not enable the MUS service.
- Similarly, Using Cloud Web Security (ScanSafe) inspection and FirePOWER module inspection cannot inspect at the same time. If an ASA found a match associated service policies which are redirecting towards both CWS and FirePOWER module, the traffic is forwarded to the ASA FirePOWER module only. If requirement is for implementation of both services, make sure that there is no overlapping in between the matching criteria for CWS and FirePOWER module.

Default Network parameters for ASA FirePOWER

Parameters	Default Value
Management IP address	System software image: 192.168.45.45/24 Boot image: 192.168.8.8/24
Gateway	System software image: none Boot image: 192.168.8.1/24
Username	admin
Password	System software image: Release 6.0 and following: Admin123 Releases prior to 6.0: Sourcefire Boot image: Admin123

Table 3-10: ASA FirePOWER default parameters

ASA FirePOWER Module (Hardware Module) Deployment in Routed Mode

The ASA FirePOWER Hardware module deployment i.e. ASA 5585-X Series has separate management interfaces from the ASA.

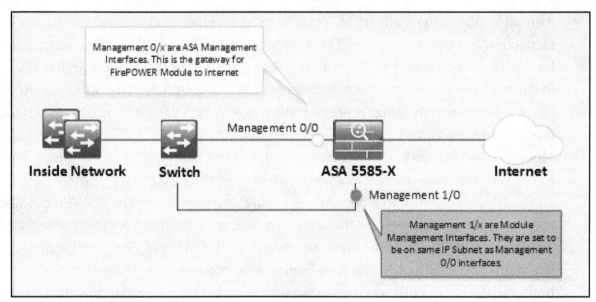

Figure 3-21: Router Mode Deployment with FirePOWER Module (Hardware)

Deployment of hardware module in routed mode requires direction of all management traffic to and from management interface, available in ASA Hardware module. Using these management interface, Management 1/0 or Management 1/1 interface traffic can be directed to in and out. FirePOWER Module also requires an internet access as these interfaces (Management 1/x) are not data interfaces, physically cable the FirePOWER module management interface to the ASA interface.

ASA FirePOWER Module (Software Module) Deployment in Routed Mode

The ASA FirePOWER Software module deployment requires ASA 5506-X to ASA 5555-X Series, using these ASA Hardware devices which has software FirePOWER module support, management interfaces i.e. Management 0/x or management 1/x can be shared where as in the Hardware deployment, it was offering a separate Management interface for FirePOWER module.

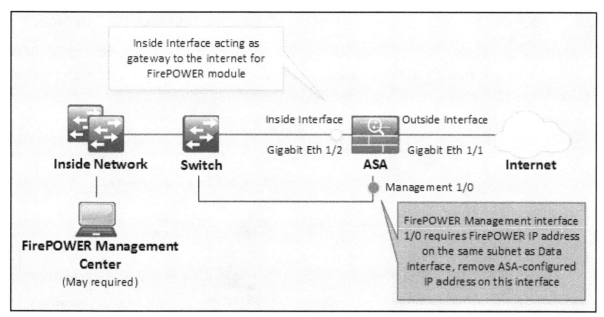

Figure 3-22: Router Mode Deployment with FirePOWER Module (Software)

Similar to deployment with hardware module, the software module deployment in routed mode also requires the management traffic passing to and from ASA FirePOWER module, entering and leaving through management interface. Management interface physical cabling is required to get internet access for FirePOWER module. In order to associate management interface to FirePOWER module, do not configure name and IP address in ASA Configuration, in this case, Management interface will be dedicated for FirePOWER Module and will not a regular ASA interface. additionally, you have to:

1. Configure ASA FirePOWER IP address i.e. on the same subnet as on ASA data interfaces.
2. Configure Data interface as gateway for FirePOWER Module.
3. Connect the configured FirePOWER management Interface to the data interface using Layer2 Switch.

ASA FirePOWER Module (Hardware Module) Deployment in Transparent Mode

Deployment guidelines for deploying ASA Firepower Module in Transparent mode are the same as for routed mode but the difference of transparent mode. ASA inside and outside interfaces are transparent, connected to inside and outside router.

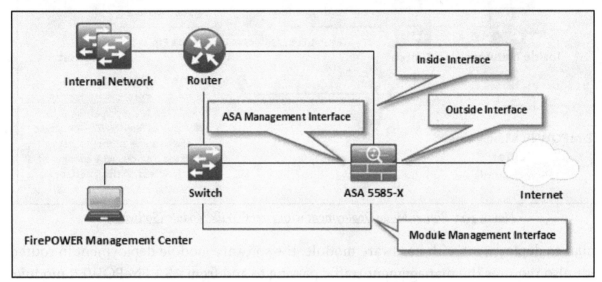

Figure 3-23: Transparent Mode Deployment with FirePOWER Module (Hardware)

If your network does not have inside router, Bridge Virtual interface can be used for ASA Management interface.

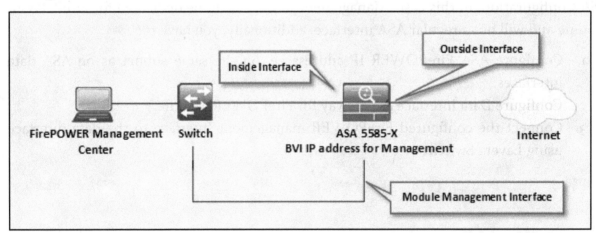

Figure 3-24: Transparent Mode Deployment with FirePOWER Module (Hardware)

ASA FirePOWER Module (Software Module) Deployment in Transparent Mode

Transparent mode with Software Module requires ASA 5506-X to ASA 5555-X, ISA 3000. These are the supported devices for software module. Configure the Transparent mode on ASA along with Management interface configured with ASA Management IP address and FirePOWER modules IP address.

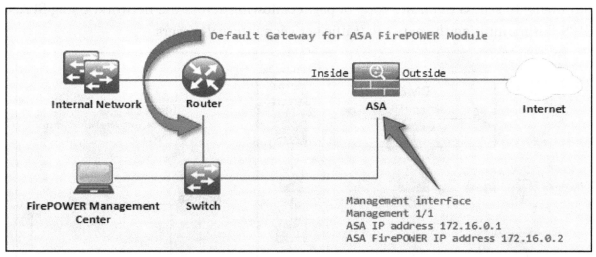

Figure 3-25: Transparent Mode Deployment with FirePOWER Module (Software)

In case no internal Router is required, deployment can be done using BVI interface for ASA Management as shown below:

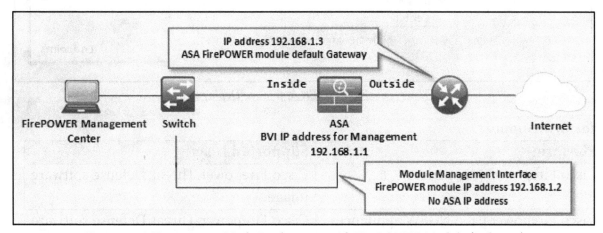

Figure 3-26: Transparent Mode Deployment with FirePOWER Module (Software)

Cisco FirePOWER Appliance Deployment

FirePOWER system deployment scenario requires Physical FirePOWER Appliance and a Physical Cisco FirePOWER Management Center. In the below figure, Physical appliances are deployed as NGIPS appliance. NGIPS-A and NGIPS-C are deployed in Inline mode whereas NGIPS-B is deployed as Passive device. Port Mirroring or SPAN is used traditionally to send a duplicate copy of packets flowing across the network. Using SPAN, NGIPS-B is monitoring the network traffic between internal servers.

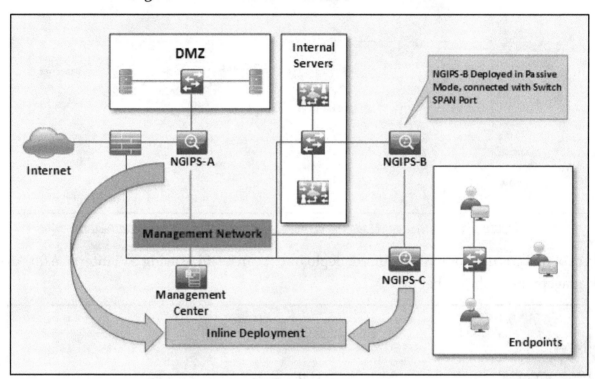

Figure 3-27: FirePOWER Appliance Deployment

Platform Support

Platform	Supported Image
Cisco Firepower 4100 Series	Cisco Firepower Threat Defense software image
Cisco Firepower 9300 NGFW appliances	Cisco Firepower Threat Defense software image
Cisco FirePOWER 8000 Series	FirePOWER software image
Cisco FirePOWER 7000 Series	FirePOWER software image
Cisco 4000 Series	FirePOWER software image
G2 Integrated Services Routers (ISR)	FirePOWER software image

Table 3-11: Cisco FirePOWER Appliances

Cisco FirePOWER Virtual Appliance Deployment

Cisco Firepower Virtual Appliance deployment offers 64-bit virtual Firepower Management Center package and virtual devices for the VMware vSphere and VMware vCloud Director. Virtual appliances by default uses e1000 interfaces i.e. 1 Gbit/s, or you can replace the default e1000 interfaces with vmxnet3 interfaces i.e. 10 Gbit/s. VMware Tools can also be configured to improve the performance and management of your virtual appliances.

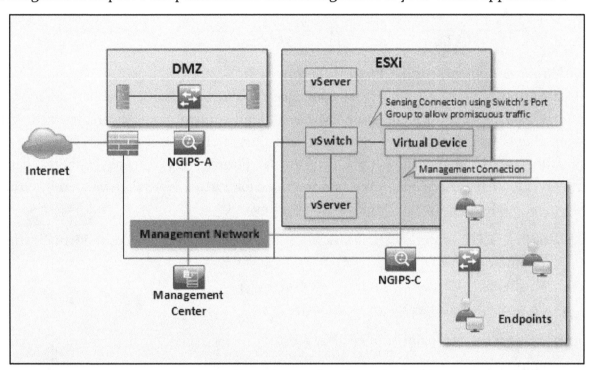

Figure 3-28: FirePOWER Virtual Appliance Deployment

Using the same scenario as for Physical appliance deployment, for virtualization, internal servers are virtualized along with FirePOWER appliance into Virtual machines. Two separate virtual Network Interface Cards vNIC are used for vSwitch and Virtual appliance as virtual appliance requires management network connection as well. Virtualized appliance is connected with switch through port group that allow promiscuous traffic.

In virtual deployment, 64-bit Cisco Firepower Management Center Virtual and 64-bit Cisco Firepower NGIPSv managed devices can be deployed to ESXi hosts using VMware vCenter or VMware vCloud Director. A virtualized Cisco FirePOWER Management Center can manage physically deployed FirePOWER devices and Cisco ASA with FirePOWER module whereas Cisco FirePOWER Management Center appliance can manage Virtualized devices. Virtual appliances do not support some services and features which are supported in Hardware based deployment.

Setting	Default	Adjustable Settings
Memory	8 GB	yes
Virtual CPU	4	up to 8
Hard disk Provisioned Size	40 GB (NGIPSv) 250 GB (FirePOWER Management Center Virtual)	no

Table 3-12: Cisco FirePOWER Virtual Appliance Guidelines

Guidelines & Limitations for Virtual Deployment

Virtualization requires 64-bit virtual appliance on VMware Esxi 5.5 using vSphere 5.5, VMware Esxi 5.1 using vSphere 5.1 or VMware vCloud Director 5.1. VMware Workstation, player, Server and fusion do not support and identify this OVF package. The Virtual Appliance can be deployed using Open Virtual Format (OVF) using vSphere client. FirePOWER Virtual Appliance OVF is introduces for Virtual Hardware version 7. Other than these guidelines, Virtual Deployment requires

- 64-bit CPU, Intel Virtualization Technology (VT) or AMD Virtualization Technology (AMD-V)
- Must enable Virtualization from BIOS settings
- Compatible interfaces with Host devices.

Limitations for the deployment of NGIPSv are

- Motion is not supported.
- Cloning a virtual machine is not supported.
- Restoring a virtual machine with snapshot is not supported.
- Restoring a backup is not supported.

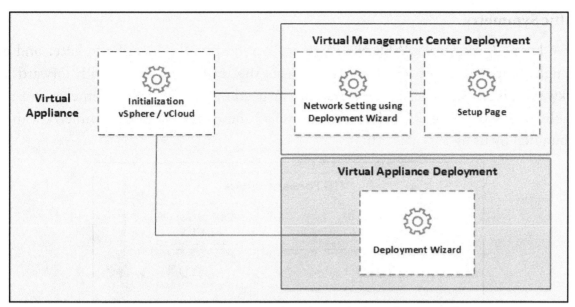

Figure 3-29: FirePOWER Virtual Appliance (VI) Configuration flow

OVF deployment on Virtual infrastructure (VI) requires some configuration settings like password for admin accounts, and configuration for communication with the network. Deployment over VI offers setup wizard for configuration.

OVF deployment on Esxi (VMware) requires configuration settings and installation process through Command line interface (CLI) through Virtual Appliance Console.

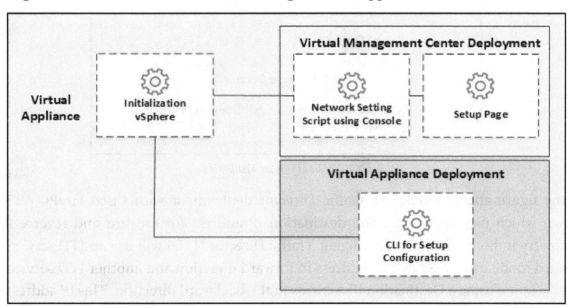

Figure 3-30: FirePOWER Virtual Appliance (ESXi) Configuration flow

Traffic Symmetry

As we know, Cisco FirePOWER NGIPS typically requires all the traffic to enter and exit through its management interfaces. It inspects the traffic flowing in both forward and backward directions. Due to this Stateful inspection, traffic flow symmetry must be established and maintained for operations ad functions. Traffic symmetry can be maintained by using ITD algorithms.

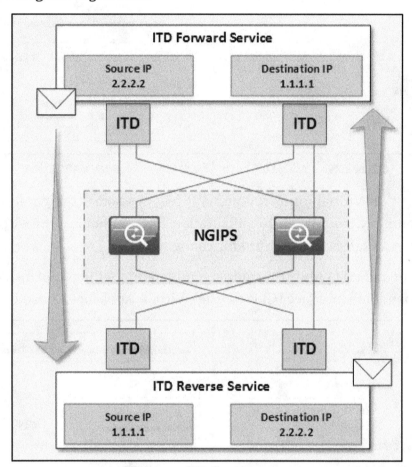

Figure 3-31: ITD flow symmetry

In the figure above, Intelligent Traffic Director deployment with Cisco FirePOWER is shown which uses the source and destination IP address for forward and reverse flow symmetry in both directions. Intelligent Traffic Director (ITD) will use an ITD service for forward mode using a Source IP Address in forward direction and another ITD service for reverse mode using a Destination IP Address in the backward direction. This IP addressing ensures that packet flows are hashed to the same NGIPS node.

Configuring ITD along with its two separate services using the value of load-balancing parameter maintain the load balancing for both services. ITD helps to ensure that flow symmetry is maintained.

Chapter 4: Security Architectures

Technology Brief

Each and every network connected to the public internet is on the risk against advanced and emerging web threats. Web, Emails and Public internet are always a popular path for viruses and malwares to spread rapidly. This growing malicious traffic over the internet is vulnerable for all those networks that are always connected. These threats can cost the network and organization in terms of information theft, disturbance in productivity including requirement of additional security teams to penetrate the calculate the scope of spread. A real-time monitoring devices is required to monitor the incoming and outgoing web traffic continuously, which also have granular control over the network to scan, inspect the traffic against particular rules and polices which decides the intensity of the inspection and could be capable of taking certain actions against the compliance.

To prevent these spreading of malwares, a network requires a security solution which keep the network secure and protected against these continuously spreading threats all over the internet. Deployment of Security solutions that monitors the traffic continuously, provide in-depth inspection, offers advanced protection against emerging threats, ensures in-depth visibility and give more granular control over the processes helps in mitigating these threats. This solution must be capable to handle even more sophisticated threats by using Threat intelligence, filtering such as URL-Filtering, Advanced malware protection and sandboxing and other techniques. Cisco recommend appropriate security appliances, for different types of network such as Cisco IronPort appliances, Cisco FirePOWER appliances that can provide integrated security solution.

Web Security Solution

Web Security Solution offered by Cisco is the Cisco Web Security Appliance. However, it is not a single device deployment solution that can protect against all web vulnerabilities and threat and keep the network secure. WSA is deployed with the integration of other devices and cloud hosted engines that provide support and offers their advanced inspection processes and techniques to provide combined scanning against the traffic flowing across the network.

Comparing Web Security Solution Options

Comparing Web Security Solutions options such as Cisco FirePOWER Next-Generation Firewall (NGFW), Cisco Web Security Appliance (WSA) and Cisco Cloud Web Security (CWS) is discussed below in order to find the most appropriate security solution.

FirePOWER	WSA	CWS
Solution Deployment		
Inline & Passive Mode Deployment with 10GE/40GE interfaces.	WSA Appliance or Virtual deployment along with Transparent Redirection through Web Browser or WCCP.	Transparent redirection to CWS using Router, ASA, WSA or Anyconnect agent.
Anti-Virus / Anti-Malware Techniques		
Multi-layer Security with AMP & NGIPS and Anti-Malware engines for Network scanning and endpoint agents for Endpoint Security	Anti-malware scanning, Web root & McAfee, Sophos, along with integration option of Cisco AMP , Cisco CTA, Third-parties integration, along with the Support of Cisco CWS.	Malware protection using AMP engines, Anti-malwares, CTA with the Support of Cisco Security Intelligence Operations (SIO).
Web Filtering & Application Control		
Web Filtering along with Application filtering, URL Filtering, File Filtering, with AVC. Advanced Application controlling options including Port hopping, Standard & Non-Standard ports, Application protocol and Signature Identification.	URL Filtering database & cache, Adult Content Filtering, End-User Filtering, Time Based Web Filtering, Web Reputation filtering & cache, File reputation filtering and File analysis. Using AVC, control over bandwidth, Instant Messaging, AVC Activity, log files, and control over application type and behaviour.	Granular control using Dynamic Content Analysis, URL Categorization, and Web Reputation filtering.
Global Threat Intelligence		
Cisco SIO and Sourcefire Vulnerability Research Team (VRT) integration through global intelligence	Cisco SIO and Sourcefire Vulnerability Research Team (VRT) integration through global intelligence	SIO and VRT intelligence feed with third part options and community support and public and

platform Cisco Collective Security Intelligence (CSI) which includes resources such as AMP, Microsoft, Snort, ClamAV communities and other intelligence	platform Cisco Collective Security Intelligence (CSI) which includes resources such as AMP, Microsoft, Snort, ClamAV communities and other intelligence along with Web Reputation filtering and Web Usage Control.	private feed along with Web Reputation and Web Usage Control.

Table 4-01: Comparing Web Security Solution

Cisco Web Security Appliance (WSA) Security Solution

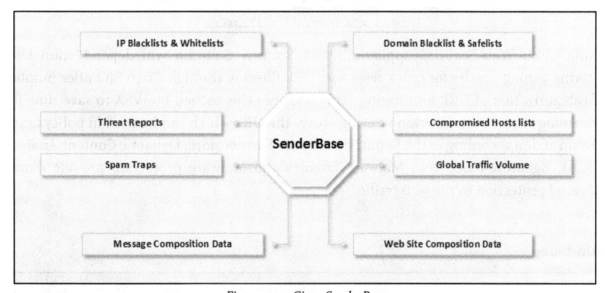

Figure 4-01: Cisco SenderBase

Cisco IronPort devices such as Cisco Web Security Appliance along with integration with SenderBase provide web security solution in combined way. Cisco Web Security Appliance (WSA) collect the information from SenderBase. This information collected from SenderBase is the intelligence report which support deciding the certain action against the compliance rules, level and severity of threats, threat level of websites, blacklisted URL and so on. Cisco IronPort devices such as WSA and ESA gain real time monitoring to provide visibility of threats, blocking of threats, spams, harmful and suspicious websites.

Enhanced Inbound Web Traffic Protection

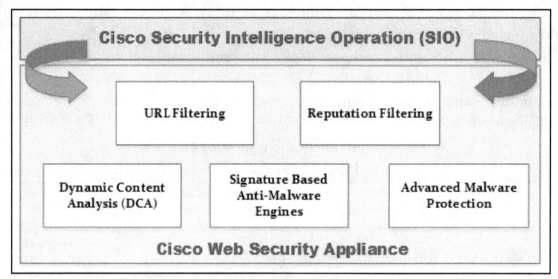

Figure 4-02: Inbound Web Protection

Using Cisco Web Security Appliance, Web Security Solution will depend upon URL filtering through cache for quick response. URL filtering through Cisco SIO offer number of categorization of URL for filtering. This response this cached by WSA to save time for upcoming requests. Reputation filtering scores the URL which can be used in policy apply certain action according to the Reputation scores. Furthermore, Dynamic Content Analysis (DCA), signature-based Anti-Malware Engines and Malware protection provide strong inbound protection to the web traffic.

Mind map

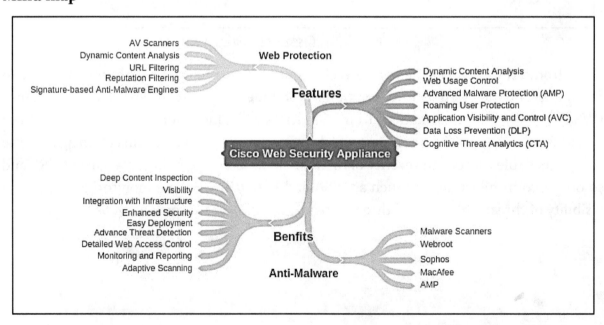

Comparing Virtual Web Security Appliance

Cisco Web Security Virtual Appliance (WSAv) requires an additional license to run its services. This license can be used for multiple, cloned virtual appliances. IP address on obtained dynamically on Management Interface, in case if DHCP is not enabled, it will continue with default management IP address i.e. 192.168.42.42/24.

Supported WSAv models for KVM Deployment

AsyncOS	Model	Disk Space	RAM	Core
AsyncOS 8.6 or later	S000V	250 GB	4 GB	1
	S100V	250 GB	6 GB	2
	S300V	1024 GB	8 GB	4
AsyncOS 10.1 or later	S600V	1024 GB	24 GB	12

Table 4-02: WSAv Models for KVM Deployment

Supported vWSA models for Esxi Deployment

AsyncOS	Model	Disk Space	RAM	Core
AsyncOS 8.6 or later	S000V	250 GB	4 GB	1
	S100V	250 GB	6 GB	2
	S300V	1024 GB	8 GB	4
AsyncOS 10.1 or later	S600V	2.4 TB	24 GB	12

Table 4-03: WSAv Models for Esxi Deployment

Supported vWSA models for Hypervisor Deployment

AsyncOS	Model	Disk Space	RAM	Core
AsyncOS 8.6 or later	S000V	250 GB	4 GB	1
	S100V	250 GB	6 GB	2
	S300V	1024 GB	8 GB	4
AsyncOS 10.1 or later	S600V	1024 GB	24 GB	12

Table 4-04: WSAv Models for Hypervisor Deployment

Cisco Web Security Appliance (WSA) is a High Performance Dedicated Hardware Appliance which is Costly in terms of purchasing an additional hardware for Web Security as compared to the deployment of Virtual Web Security Appliance (vWSA) deployed over server as an instance.

Cisco Web Security Appliance (WSA) Performance

Users	Model	Disk Space	Memory	CPU
6000 - 12000	S680	4.8 TB	32 GB	16 Core
	S670	2.7 TB	8 GB	8 Core
1500 - 6000	S380	2.4 TB	16 GB	6 Core
	S370	1.8 TB	4 GB	4 Core
< 1500	S170	500 GB	4 GB	2 Core

Table 4-05: WSA Hardware Appliance Performance Chart

Cisco Web Security Virtual Appliance (vWSA) Performance

Users	Model	Disk Space	Memory	CPU
3000 - 6000	S300V	250 GB	8 GB	4 Core
1000 - 2999	S100V	250 GB	6 GB	2 Core
< 1000	S000V	1024 GB	4 GB	1 Core

Table 4-06: WSA Virtual Appliance Performance Chart

Compatible Versions of WSA Appliance and WSAv

Source Version	Destination Version
WSA 7.5.0	WSAv 7.7.5
WSA 7.5.1	WSAv 7.7.5
WSA 7.5.2	WSAv 7.7.5
WSA 7.7.0	WSAv 7.7.5 (Directly, without Configuration Migration tool)
WSAv 7.7.5	WSAv 7.7.0

Table 4-07: WSA Compatible Versions

Configuration Migration tools is required for migration in between hardware appliance and Virtual appliance. This is a Command Line application that runs over windows 7. This tool is capable to convert the configuration file of Physical Cisco Web Security Appliance (WSA) into compatible configuration file for Virtual appliance of Cisco WSA. Similarly, WSAv configuration file can also convert for Physical WSA appliance.

CWS Connectors

CWS Features	ASA Connector	WSA Connector	IOS Connector	AnyConnect Connector	Mobile Browser
Traffic Redirection	Transparent				
SSL Tunnelling	No		GRE over IPsec (ISR-4K)	Yes (Default)	No
Whitelist	IP	IP/CIDR FQDN URL User Agent	IP URL User Agent	IP Host	IP URL Host
Supported Browser in Transparent mode	Internet Explorer				N/A
	Chrome				
	Firefox				
	Safari	-	Safari		
Supported OS in Transparent mode	Windows / OS X	Windows		Windows / OS X	iOS / Android
Supported Browser in Non-transparent mode	All			N/A	
Supported OS in Non-transparent mode	Windows / OS X / iOS			N/A	iOS / Android

Table 4-08: CWS Connectors

Cloud Web Security Connectors for IOS
Hardware Requirement for CWS Connector
- Cisco 800 Series Routers
- Cisco 1900 Series Integrated Services Router (ISR) (1905/1921/1941/1941W)
- Cisco 2900 Series Integrated Services Routers (2901/2911/2921/2951)
- Cisco 3900 Series Integrated Services Routers (3925/3925E/3945/3945E)

Cloud Web Security Connectors for ASA

Hardware Requirement for CWS Connector

- Cisco ASA 5500 and 5500-X Series with version 9.x or later can integrate with Cisco Cloud Web Security.

Cloud Web Security Connectors for WSA

Supported by both Cisco WSA Appliance and Virtual Appliance (vWSA).

Email Security Solution

Comparing Physical ESA Appliance and virtual ESA

On Premises Deployment

Cisco Email Security Appliance (ESA) is the physical hardware appliance that is deployed on premises as the security gateway that is deployed at the edge of the network after the firewall in Demilitarized zone (DMZ). All incoming traffic is directed to the appliance using incoming SMTP, to filter and forward it to internal mail server.

Virtual Deployment

Virtualization of Cisco Email Security Appliance as ESA instance can be deployed using Cisco Unified Computing System (UCS), Hypervisor, KVM and Esxi. Deployment of Virtual appliance provide equal protection and same level of security as hardware appliance. The benefit of Virtualization is to save money, complexity in terms of additional hardware, power resources and maintenance.

Configuration Migration Tool

Configuration Migration tools is required for migration in between hardware appliance and Virtual appliance. This is a Command Line application that runs over windows 7. This tool is capable to convert the configuration file of Physical Cisco Email Security Appliance (ESA) into compatible configuration file for Virtual appliance of Cisco ESA. Similarly, ESAv configuration file can also convert for Physical ESA appliance.

Source Version	Destination Version
ESA 7.6.0	ESAv 8.0.0
ESA 7.6.1	ESAv 8.0.0
ESA 7.6.2	ESAv 8.0.0
ESA 7.6.3	ESAv 8.0.0
ESA 8.0.0	ESAv 8.0.0
ESAv 8.0.0	ESA 8.0.0

Table 4-09: Compatible Version for Migration

Non-Compatible Configuration in Migration

Before uploading the converted configuration file, you must configure the following parameters. These configuration parameters cannot be transferred in Migration process between physical and virtual security appliances:

- Network settings
- Hardware-specific settings
- SaaS certificate names

Supported Virtual Appliance Model and AsyncOS version for Hypervisor

Product Name	AsyncOS Version	Model	Disk Space	RAM	Processor (Core)
Cisco Web Security Virtual Appliance	AsyncOS 11.0 or Later	S000V	250 GB	4 GB	1
		S100V	250 GB	6 GB	2
		S300V	1024 GB	8 GB	4
		S600V	1024 GB	24 GB	12

Table 4-10: Hypervisor supported model of ESAv

Supported Virtual Appliance Model and AsyncOS version for KVM

Product Name	AsyncOS Version	Model	Disk Space	RAM	Processor (Core)
Cisco Email Security Virtual Appliance	AsyncOS 11.0 or Later	C000V	200 GB	4 GB	1 Core
		C100V	200 GB	6 GB	2 Core
		C300V	500 GB	8 GB	4 Core
		C600V	500 GB	8 GB	8 Core
	AsyncOS 10.0 or Later	C000V	200 GB	4 GB	1 Core
		C100V	200 GB	6 GB	2 Core
		C300V	500 GB	8 GB	4 Core
		C600V	500 GB	8 GB	8 Core

Table 4-11: KVM supported model of ESAv

Supported Virtual Appliance Model and AsyncOS version for Esxi

Product Name	Model	Disk Space	RAM	Processor (Core)
Cisco Email Security Virtual Appliance	C000V (Evaluation)	200 GB	4 GB	1 Core
	C100V	200 GB	6 GB	2 Core
	C300V	500 GB	8 GB	4 Core
	C600V	500 GB	8 GB	8 Core

Table 4-12: ESXi supported model of ESAv

Compatible VMware Esxi Version to AsyncOS version

AsyncOS Version	VMWare ESXi Version
AsyncOS 11.x (For Email)	6.0
AsyncOS 11.x (For Management)	
AsyncOS 10.1 and later (For Web)	
AsyncOS 11.x (For Email)	5.0, 5.1, and 5.5
AsyncOS 11.x (For Management)	
AsyncOS 9.x and later (For Web)	
AsyncOS 10.x (For Email)	6.0
AsyncOS 10.x (For Management)	
AsyncOS 10.1 and later (For Web)	
AsyncOS 10.x (For Email)	5.0, 5.1, and 5.5
AsyncOS 10.x (For Management)	
AsyncOS 9.x and later (For Web)	
AsyncOS 9.x (For Email)	5.0, 5.1, and 5.5
AsyncOS 9.x (For Management)	
AsyncOS 8.7 and later (For Web)	
AsyncOS 8.5 (For Web)	5.0 and 5.1
AsyncOS 8.4 (For Management)	
AsyncOS 8.5.x (For Email)	4.x, 5.0, and 5.1
AsyncOS 8.0.x (For Web)	
AsyncOS 8.0 (For Email)	4.x and 5.0
AsyncOS 7.7.5 (For Web)	

Table 4-13: ESXi supported AsyncOS Versions

Comparing Performance Specification

ESA Virtual Appliance				
Deployment	Model	Disk	Memory	Core
Evaluation Only	ESAv C000v	200 GB	4 GB	1
Up to 1000 Users (Small Deployment)	ESAv C100v	200 GB	6 GB	2
Up to 5000 users (Medium Deployment)	ESAv C300v	500 GB	8 GB	4
Service Provider or Large Enterprise	ESAv C600v	500 GB	8 GB	8

Table 4-14: ESA Performance Chart

ESA Hardware Appliance				
Deployment	**Model**	**Disk Space**	**RAM**	**Core**
Large Deployment	ESA C690	2.4 TB	32 GB	6 Core
Large Deployment	ESA C690X	4.8 TB	32 GB	6 Core
Large Deployment	ESA C680	1.8 TB	32 GB	6 Core
Medium Deployment	ESA C390	1.2 TB	16 GB	6 Core
Medium Deployment	ESA C380	1.2 TB	16 GB	6 Core
Small Deployment	ESA C190	1.2 TB	8 GB	6 Core
Small Deployment	ESA C170	500 GB	4 GB	2 Core

Table 4-15: ESAv Performance Chart

Mind Map

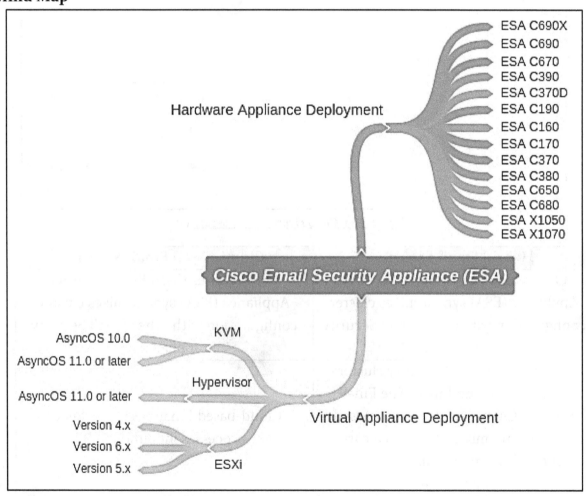

Cisco Hybrid Email Security

Cisco Hybrid Email Security solution is the combined security solution for Email traffic based on On-Premises Email Security Appliance and Cloud-based Email Security Appliances. Cloud-based Email Security Infrastructure is typically used for inbound Email traffic, whereas On-Premises Email Security Appliance is used to provide additional layer of security providing along with advanced content filtering and Email encryption techniques.

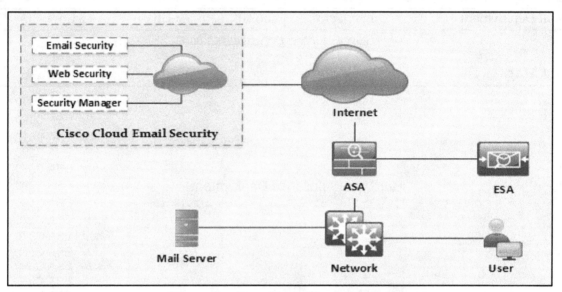

Figure 4-03: Cisco Hybrid Email Security

Hybrid Email Security	Cloud-based Email Security
On-Premises Cisco Email Security Appliance (ESA) synchronizes cluster configuration with other Email Security appliances.	On-Premises Cisco Email Security Appliance (ESA) synchronizes cluster configuration with other Email Security appliances.
Cloud-based Email Security cluster processes inbound mail. The Email Security Cluster sends the processed mail to on-premises ESA, which carries out additional filtering & policies inspection	Cloud-based Email Security cluster processes inbound mail.
Cloud-based Security Management Appliance collect the reports and tracking information from the Cloud Email Security appliances and from on-premises Email Security appliance (ESA).	Cloud-based Security Management Appliance collect the reports and tracking information from the Cloud Email Security appliances.

Cloud-based Security Management appliance is the central quarantine for spam	Cloud-based Security Management appliance is the central quarantine for spam
Mail that is filtered based on policy is quarantined on the Cisco Security Management appliance.	Mail that is filtered is centrally quarantined.
On-premises ESA Processes Inbound and Outbound Emails providing Filtering and Encryption. On-premises ESA forwards the incoming processed mails to server, processes the outbound mail from server, providing filtering and encryption.	Cloud Processes Inbound and Outbound Emails providing Filtering and Encryption. Processed mail are sent directly to the server.

Table 4-16: Cisco Hybrid Email Security

Cisco FirePOWER Solution

Virtual Routed Interface

Routed interfaces can be configured as either physical routed interface as well as logical or Virtual Routed interface. Physical Routed interface can handle untagged traffic whereas logical routed interface can handle VLAN tagged traffic. Layer 3 deployment of routed interfaces requires association of external physical interface to the physical or logical routed interface. If interfaces are not associated, traffic will be dropped.

Configuring Virtual Routed interface

Configuration
1. Choose **Devices** > **Device Management.**
2. Click **Edit** Icon

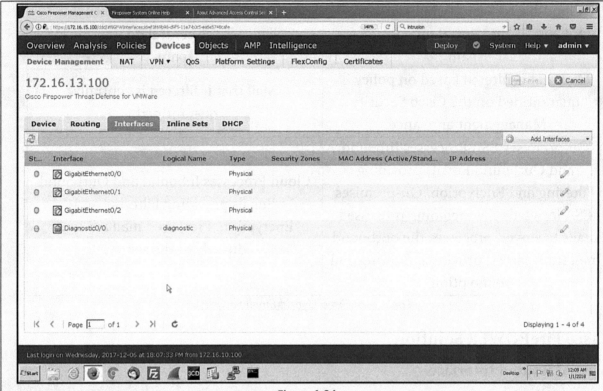

Figure 4-04

3. Click **Add Interface**
4. Click **Routed**

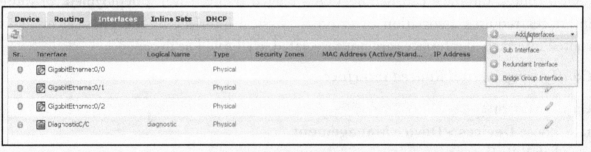

Figure 4-05

```
Options may differ in different versions
```

5. Select associated Physical interface from drop down option
6. Enter VLAN tag
7. If required, configure Security zone option
8. Specify Virtual Router
9. Check the **Enable** Checkbox to allow the interface to handle the traffic
10. Select MTU

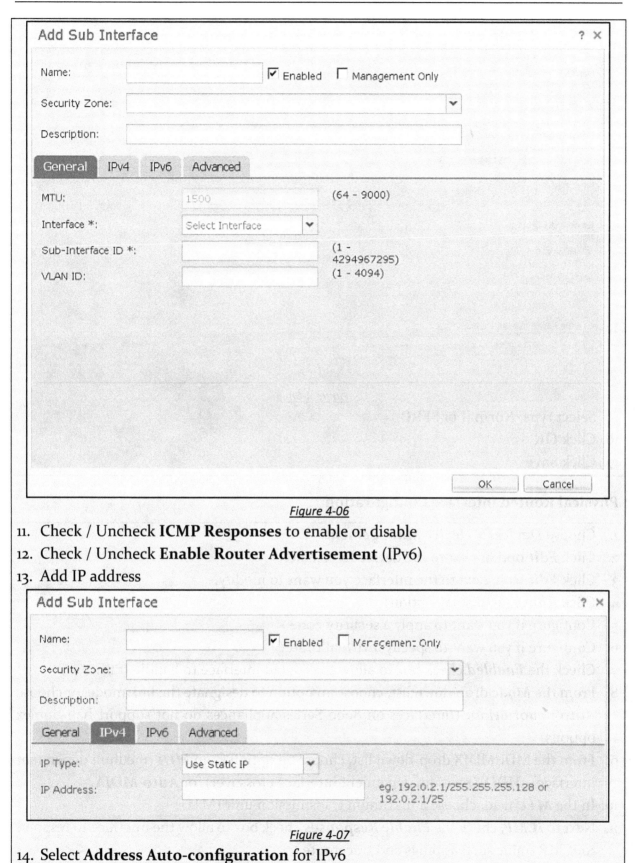

Figure 4-06

11. Check / Uncheck **ICMP Responses** to enable or disable
12. Check / Uncheck **Enable Router Advertisement** (IPv6)
13. Add IP address

Figure 4-07

14. Select **Address Auto-configuration** for IPv6

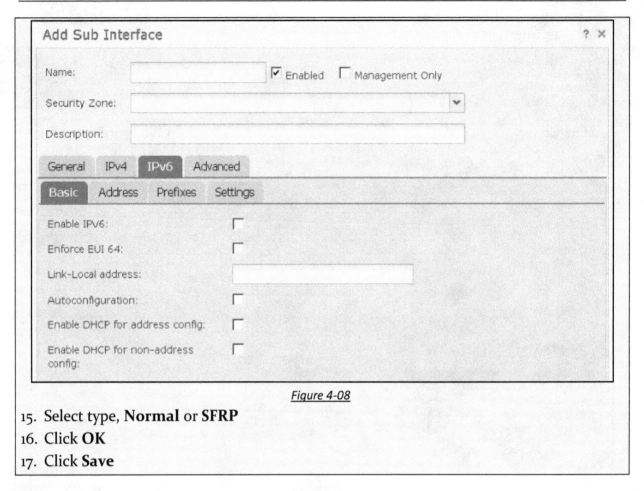

Figure 4-08

15. Select type, **Normal** or **SFRP**
16. Click **OK**
17. Click **Save**

Physical Routed Interface Configuration

1. Choose *Devices > Device Management.*
2. Click *Edit* option next to the device to be edited
3. Click *Edit* icon, next to the interface you want to modify.
4. Click *Routed* to display options.
5. Configure if you want to apply a security zone
6. Configure if you want to specify a virtual router
7. Check the *Enabled* check box to allow the routed interface to handle traffic.
8. From the *Mode* drop-down list, choose an option to designate the link mode, or choose *Auto-negotiation.* (Interfaces on 8000 Series appliances do not support half-duplex options)
9. From the MDI/MDIX drop-down list, choose an option from *MDI* (medium dependent interface), *MDIX* (medium dependent interface crossover), or *Auto-MDIX.*
10. In the *MTU* field, choose a maximum transmission unit (MTU)
11. Next to *ICMP,* check the *Enable Responses* check box to allow the interface to respond to ICMP traffic such as pings and traceroute.

12. Next to IPv6 NDP, check the **Enable Router Advertisement** check box to enable the interface to broadcast router advertisements.

13. To add an IP address, click **Add.**

14. In the **Address** field, enter the routed interface's IP address and subnet mask using CIDR notation.

15. If your organization uses IPv6 addresses and you want to set the IP address of the interface automatically, check the **Address Auto configuration** check box next to the IPv6 field.

16. For **Type,** choose either **Normal** or **SFRP.**

17. Click **OK.**

18. Add an IP address

19. Add ARP entry

20. Click **OK.**

21. Click **Save.**

Virtual Switched Interface

Switched Interface Configuration can be configured in either physical or logical. In a Layer 2 scenario, Physical Switched Interface and Logical Switched interface can be configured for dealing the VLAN traffic, Physical Switched interface for untagged VLAN traffic and Logical Switched interface for designated VLAN tags. If external physical interface received untagged traffic and physical switched interface is not configured, the packet will be dropped. Similarly, tagged traffic will be dropped if virtual switched interface is not configured.

Configuring Virtual Switched interface

Configuration
1. Choose **Devices > Device Management**.
2. Click the **Edit** icon
3. Click **Add interface**
4. Select Associated Physical Interface which receive VLAN tagged traffic from Interface Drop down list
5. Enter the VLAN tag value
6. If required, Select Security Zone
7. Associate the Switched Interface to the Virtual Switch
8. Click Enable to allow the interface to handle the traffic
9. Enter MTU
10. Click **Save**

Hybrid Interface

Hybrid interface is the logical interface in FirePOWER devices which bridges traffic between virtual routers and virtual switches. If IP traffic is received on the hybrid interface, the interface handles it as Layer 3 traffic. It will either process the traffic according to the destination IP address. If the hybrid interface receives layer 2 traffic, it will handle it as virtual Switched traffic. FirePOWER NGIPSv is not capable of logical hybrid interfaces.

Configuration of Hybrid interface requires association of Hybrid interface to both Virtual Switch and Virtual Router. If Hybrid interface is not associated with both virtual devices (virtual router and virtual switch), interface will not entertain routing.

Logical Hybrid Interface requires association with Virtual Router and Virtual Switches to entertain the incoming traffic to bridge between layer 2 and 3. Only one Hybrid interface can be associated with the virtual Switch whereas virtual router can support multiple hybrid interface. These hybrid interface can be configured for Cisco Redundancy protocol (SFRP). In order to prevent ICMP responses, disabling ICMP Enable Responses is not enough. To prevent these responses, manually add a rule to access control policy for dropping the packet incoming to hybrid interface with ICMP protocol or enable Inspect Local Router Traffic option.

Configuring Hybrid Interface

Configuration
1. Choose ***Devices > Device Management.***
2. Click ***Edit.***
3. choose ***Add Logical Interface*** from the Add drop-down menu.
4. Select ***Hybrid*** to display the hybrid interface options.
5. Enter the Name of Hybrid interface.
6. Choose an existing virtual router, choose None, or choose ***New*** to add a new virtual router from the Virtual Router drop-down list.
7. Choose an existing virtual switch, choose ***None***, or choose ***New*** to add a new virtual switch from the Virtual Switch drop-down list.
8. Check the ***Enabled*** check box to allow the hybrid interface to handle traffic.
9. In the ***MTU*** field, Enter a maximum transmission unit (MTU).
10. Next to ICMP, Check / Uncheck the ***Enable Responses*** check box to allow the interface to respond to ICMP traffic such as pings and traceroute.
11. Next to IPv6 NDP, check the ***Enable Router Advertisement*** if you added IPv6 addresses.
12. To add an IP address, click ***Add.***
13. For Type, choose either ***Normal*** or ***SFRP.***
14. If you chose SFRP for Type, set options as described in SFRP.

15. Click **OK**.
16. Click **Save.**

Chapter 5: Troubleshooting, Monitoring and Reporting Tools

Cisco Web Security Appliance (WSA)

WSA Policy Trace Tool

Policy Trace tool is a very helpful tool which provides sufficient support for troubleshooting issues related to policies configured on the device. The Policy Trace tool is capable to evaluate the process of web proxy processes which are enforced over client request. This tool is used for tracing the request of client by mean of troubleshooting issues and debugging the process step to identify and locate the problem. Policy Trace Tool can perform basic tracing as well as with advance options. These tracing requests by tracing tool are not logged or reported in reporting database.

Policy Trace Tool can perform its action against the requests that are associated with the policies which are used by Web Proxy such as Access Control policies, Encrypted HTTPS policies, Routing, Data Security and Outbound Scanning policies. All External policies which are not related to Proxy Server will not by entertained such as SOCKS or External Data Loss Prevention Policies.

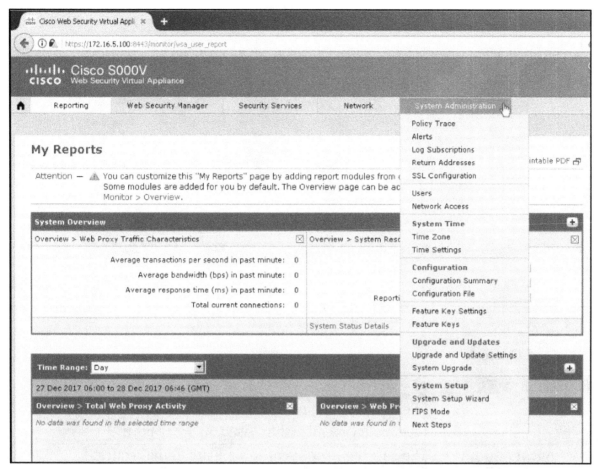

Figure 5-01: Policy Trace tool

Implementing Policy Trace Tool

Basic Policy Trace
1. Choose System Administration > Policy Trace.
2. Enter the URL to trace, in the Destination URL field.

3. Enter additional emulation parameters (Optional):
      a- Client Source IP Address
      b- Authentication / Identification Credentials

4. Click Find Policy Match

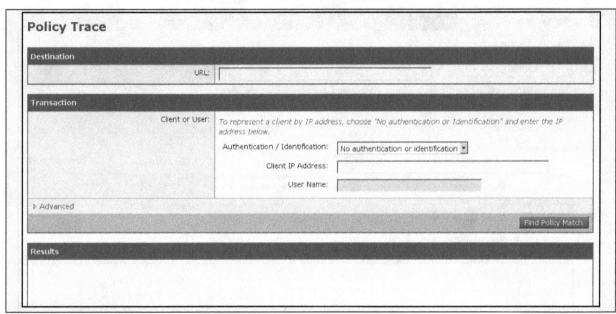

Figure 5-02

Advanced Options

Option	Description
Proxy Port	Select a specific proxy port to use for the trace request to test policy membership based on proxy port.
User Agent	Specify the User Agent to simulate in the request.
Time of Request	Specify the Date and Time of day to simulate in the request.
Upload File	Choose a local file to simulate uploading in the request.
Object Size	Enter the size of the request object in bytes. You can enter K, M, or G to represent Kilobytes, Megabytes, or Gigabytes.
MIME Type	Enter the MIME type.
Anti-malware Scanning Verdicts	To override a Webroot, McAfee, or Sophos scanning verdict, choose the specific type of verdict to be overridden.

Table 5-01: Policy Trace Tool Advance Options

WSA Reporting Function

Cisco Web Security Appliance (WSA) is capable of generating high-level reports. These High-level reports are monitored by the administrator or the IT team to determine the functions and processes that are running across the network. These reports also provide detailed view of traffic related information such as domain, user, or category. These reporting function can be used for specific interval of time in order to view system activity over a certain period of time. Additionally, you can schedule these reporting, and run them at regular intervals.

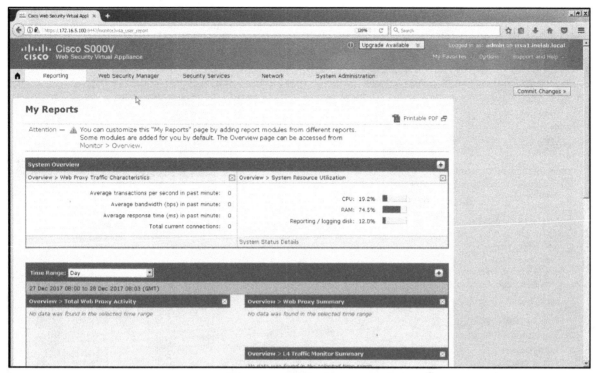

Figure 5-03: WSA Reporting

WSA Reporting Pages

Cisco WSA offers the number of reports listed below:

1. **Application Visibility**

    You can scroll down to **Reporting > Application Visibility** to get information related to the applications and Application types which are being used by blocked by the inspection of Application Visibility & Control (AVC).

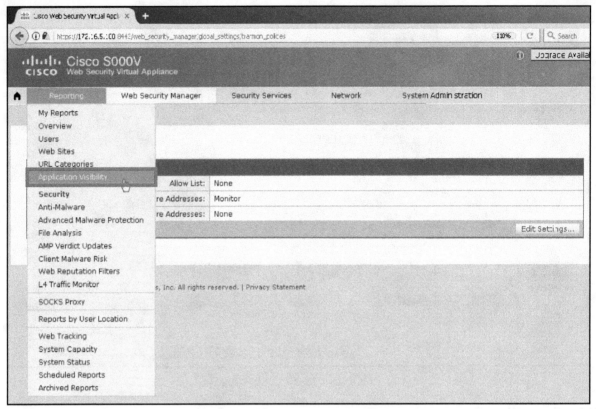

Figure 5-04: Application Visibility

It contains the list of top applications by total transactions, list of top applications by blocked transactions, list of matched applications, and applications type.

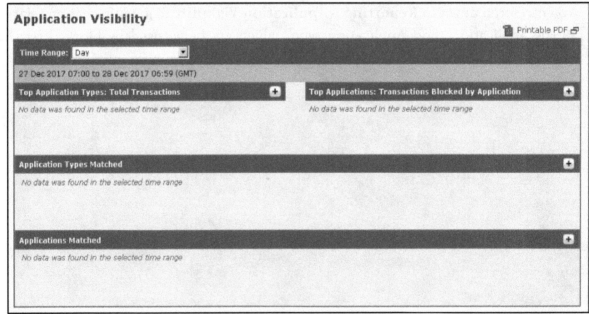

Figure 5-05: WSA Application Visibility

2. **Anti-Malware**

   The **Reporting > Anti-Malware** page contain Anti-Malware reporting, which allows monitoring and identifying malware detected by the Cisco Distributed Virtual Switch (DVS) engine. It lists the top malware categories detected by Cisco DVS engine, Malware categories they are associated to, and information of particular malware threat.

3. **Archived Reports**

   Archived Report can be navigated to **Reporting > Archived Reports** page. Archived reports list available archived reports. These reports are listed by the name of report with a link which display the details of that report.

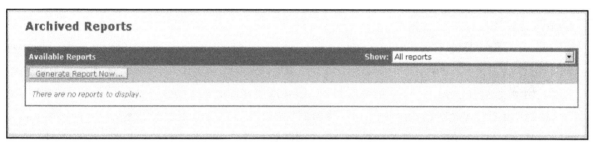

Figure 5-06: WSA Archived Reporting

4. **Client Malware Risk**

   Client Malware Risk Page at **Reporting > Client Malware Risk** is associated to security-related reporting which can be used to monitor client malware risk activities. This report lists client IP addresses, involved in frequent malicious connections which are identified by the L4 Traffic Monitor (L4TM).

5. **L4 Traffic Monitor**

   L4 Traffic Monitor Page at **Reporting > L4 Traffic Monitor** is associated with security-related reporting which can be used to get information regarding Malware ports and malicious sites. This report lists client IP addresses, involved in frequent malicious connections which are identified by the L4 Traffic Monitor (L4TM). It lists top client IP addresses involved in malicious connections in graphical format, malware sites in graphical format, Source Client IP addresses, malware ports and domains of Malware sites.

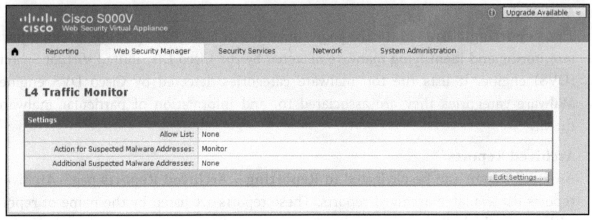

Figure 5-07: L4 Traffic Monitor

6. **Overview**

When you Scroll to Overview page of report i.e. go to **Reporting > Overview**, the page will display the information regarding the activities running on Web Security Appliance including graphs, Summary and tables. Overview page is focused for System overview containing the Web Proxy Traffic Characteristic, System Resource Utilization section as well as Summary information including Total Web Proxy Activity, Web Proxy Summary, L4 Traffic Monitor Summary, Suspect transactions summary, Total Transactions, URL Categories, Malware Categories blocked or monitored, and Users which re blocked or monitored.

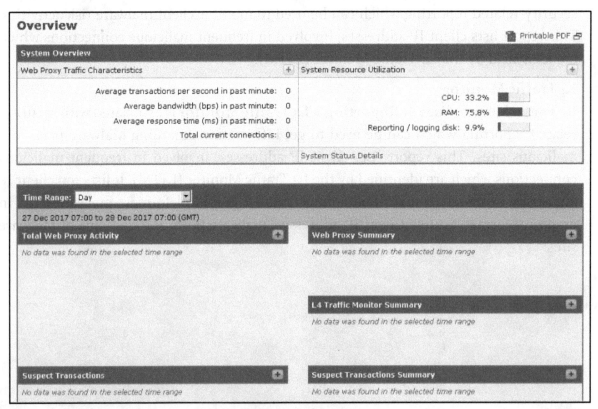

Figure 5-08: Overview

7. **URL Categories**

   URL category page shows information regarding list of matched URL categories, Blocked URL categories, Warned URL Categories, and list of total URL categories involved in transactions in graphical format.

8. **Users**

   When you scroll to User Reporting page i.e. go to **Reporting > User**, the page will display the number of links which provide Web traffic information associated with the individual users. This traffic information includes how long the user accesses the internet, number of time a specific user hit the specific URL including bandwidth details user occupied. You can refine the results using the Time range feature as well. User page contain list of users which are on the top for blocked transactions, list of users occupying the most bandwidth. Additionally, the page also has statistics of individual users.

9. **Web Sites**

   Reporting > Web Site page offers the aggregated information of activities running on Web Security Appliance such as list of domain which are visited in graphical format, graph of domain which are blocked, and domains matched.

10. **AMP, AMP Verdict Updates & File Analysis**

    Advanced Malware Protection Reporting page shows the files of threat that are identified by file reputation service. This displays all instances of the file in Web Tracking that were encountered within the maximum available time range, regardless of the time range selected for the report. Similarly results associated to File Analysis and AMP Verdict Update are shown on their respective pages.

    The following are also some other reporting pages which show information of activities running on Web Security Appliance associated to these categories.

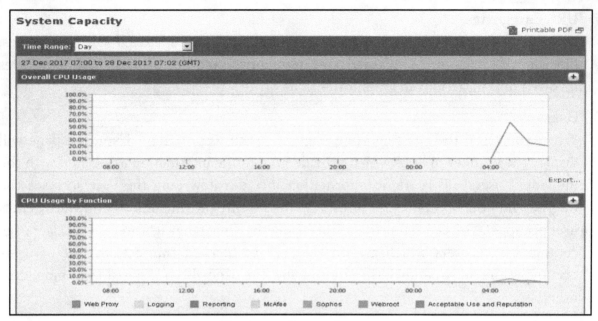

Figure 5-09: System Capacity

11. Web Reputation Filters
12. Web Tracking
13. Reports by User Location
14. Scheduled Reports
15. SOCKS Proxy
16. System Capacity
17. System Status

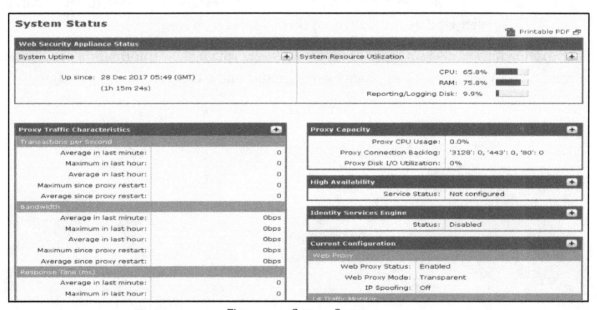

Figure 5-10: System Status

WSA Report Pages Options

These reports pages provide detailed information of system activities and other information. Reports showing the result support different options to examine the data and view with different aspects.

1. **Change the time range:**
    Time Range option allows updating of the results displayed according to the configured Time range. You can use pre-defined Time ranges as well as Custom Time range including:

    - Hour
    - Day
    - Week
    - Month
    - Yesterday
    - Custom Range

2. **Search**
    Some Report pages include the search option. Search feature can be used to filter the specific data from reports. Search option include the following parameters:

    - Users
    - Web Sites
    - URL Categories
    - Application Visibility
    - Client Malware Risk

3. **Selection of Data to display in Chart**
    Report pages containing the Chart commonly use the Referenced data in which you select your desired data for chart. If the page contains more than one chart, you can modify each of them.

4. **Export of Reports.**
    You can generate custom reports as well and export these reports to external file in different formats.

Centralized Reporting

Using Centralized Reporting, Cisco Web Security Appliance (WSA) can send its reports to the Centralized Reporting Center i.e. Cisco Content Security Management Appliance. Content Security Management Appliance can collect and aggregate and record reports from multiple Web Security Appliances. Web Security Appliance can only store its

information and reports associated with that appliance only. If centralized management is enabled, WSA only record System Capacity and System Status data.

Scheduled Reports

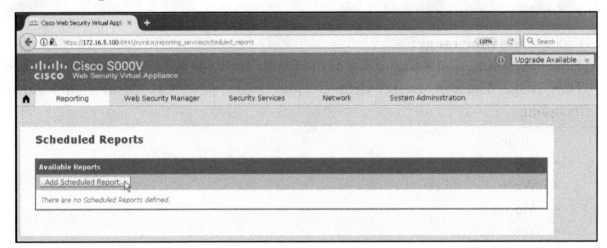

Figure 5-11: WSA Scheduled Reports

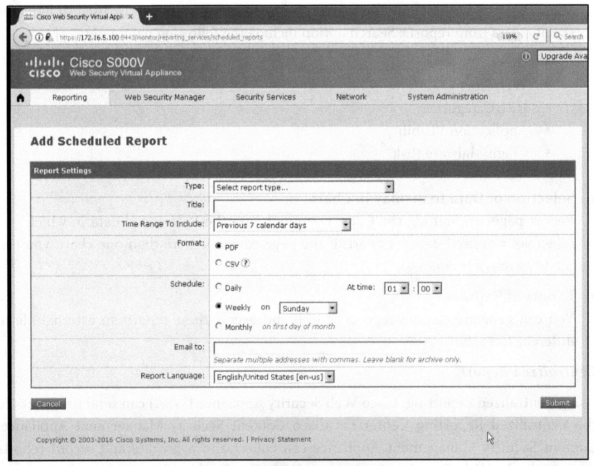

Figure 5-12: WSA Scheduled Reports

You can configure the following reports to schedule on a daily, weekly or monthly basis.

- Overview
- Users
- Web Sites
- URL Categories
- Application Visibility
- Anti-Malware
- Advanced Malware Protection
- Advanced Malware Protection Verdict Updates
- Client Malware Risk
- Web Reputation Filters
- L4 Traffic Monitor
- SOCKS Proxy
- Reports by User Location
- System Capacity
- My Dashboard

Troubleshooting Using CLI Tools

Whoami Command

This Command "whoami" display the username along with full name and the associated group of the user which is currently logged in to the device

Syntax: **whoami**

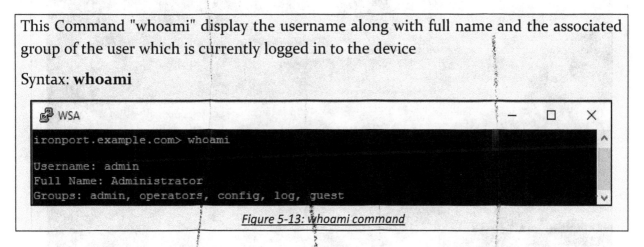

Figure 5-13: whoami command

Traceroute Command

This Command "traceroute" test the connectivity to the specific destination from that appliance and show results hop by hop.

Syntax: **traceroute**

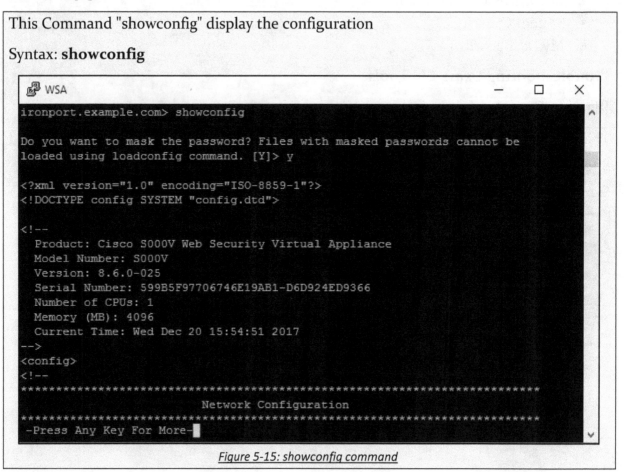

Figure 5-14: traceroute command

Show configuration Command

This Command "showconfig" display the configuration

Syntax: **showconfig**

```
ironport.example.com> showconfig

Do you want to mask the password? Files with masked passwords cannot be
loaded using loadconfig command. [Y]> y

<?xml version="1.0" encoding="ISO-8859-1"?>
<!DOCTYPE config SYSTEM "config.dtd">

<!--
   Product: Cisco S000V Web Security Virtual Appliance
   Model Number: S000V
   Version: 8.6.0-025
   Serial Number: 599B5F97706746E19AB1-D6D924ED9366
   Number of CPUs: 1
   Memory (MB): 4096
   Current Time: Wed Dec 20 15:54:51 2017
-->
<config>
<!--
*********************************************************************
                      Network Configuration
*********************************************************************
-Press Any Key For More-
```

Figure 5-15: showconfig command

Diagnostic Command

This Command "diagnostic" is used to check information such as RAID Disk, Cache information connectivity test to other mail servers.

Syntax: **diagnostic *[Sub-command]***

Sub-Commands: Net, Proxy & Reporting

Net	:	Network diagnostic
Proxy	:	Proxy Debugging
Reporting	:	Reporting Utility

```
WSA                                              —    □    ×
ironport.example.com> diagnostic


Choose the operation you want to perform:
- NET - Network Diagnostic Utility.
- PROXY - Proxy Debugging Utility.
- REPORTING - Reporting Utilities.
[]>
```

Figure 5-16: diagnostic command

Grep Command

This Command "grep" is used to Search specific information such as text in a log file.

Syntax: **grep [-C count] [-e regex] [-i] [-p] [-t] [regex] log_name**

Command options:

-C	:	Provide number of lines around grep content
-e	:	Enter Regular Expression
-i	:	Ignore case sensitivity
-p	:	Paginate the output
-t	:	Run the command over the tail of log file
regex	:	Enter a regular Expression

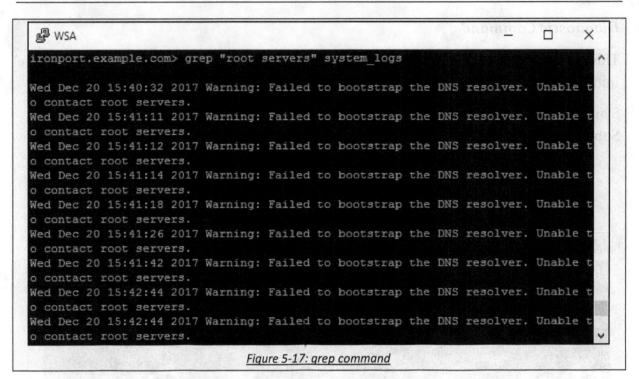

Figure 5-17: grep command

Technical Support Command

This Command "techsupport" offers the temporary connection to Cisco Support, it allows the support to access the system for technical support.

Syntax: **techsupport**

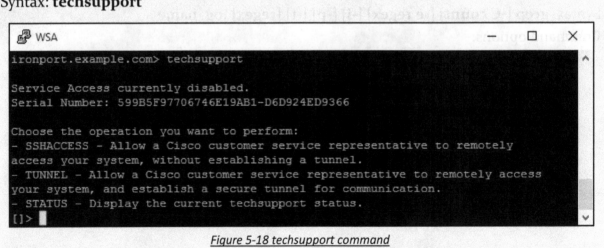

Figure 5-18 techsupport command

Tail Command

This Command "tail" display end of log file. It can also accept with File name or number parameter along with syntax.

Syntax: **tail**

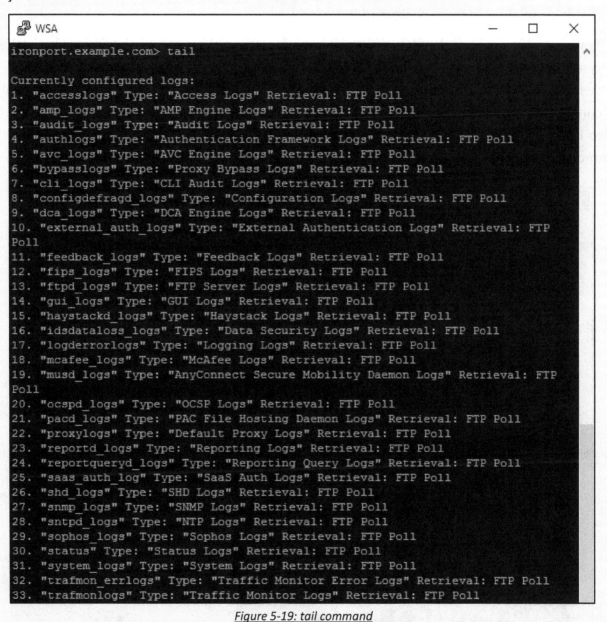

Figure 5-19: tail command

Cisco Email Security Appliance (ESA)

ESA Policy Trace Tool

Similar to Policy Trace Tool in WSA, Cisco Email Security Appliance (ESA) offer Trace CLI command and GUI Trace feature. Scroll down to the **System Administration** > **Trace** page that is equivalent to trace command in the CLI.

Trace service ensures the debugging of messages flow throughout the network by the system by sending a test message. The Trace feature emulates a test packet towards the destination, feed summary of events been "triggered" or affected by the current configuration of the ESA. The test message emulated by the Trace tool is not actually sent to the destination. This feature also helps to diagnose the issues in committed as well as uncommitted changes. The Trace tool is not effective for testing of File reputation service.

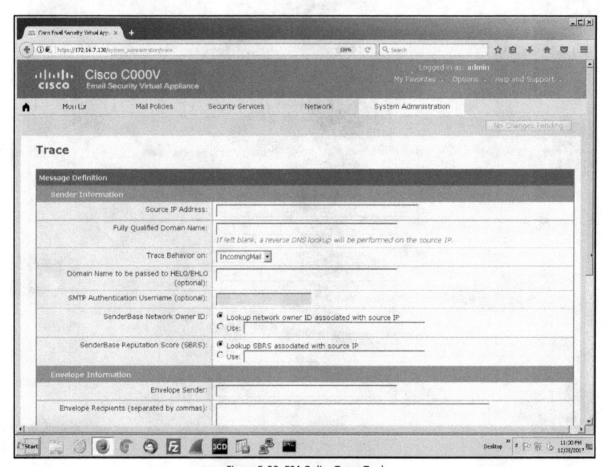

Figure 5-20: ESA Policy Trace Tool

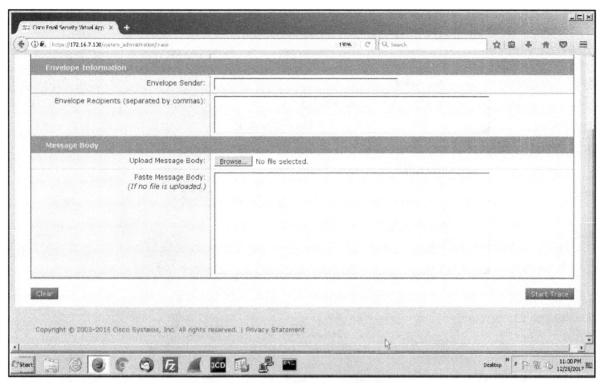

Figure 5-21 ESA Policy Trace Tool

ESA Trace Tool Page and CLI Inputs

Input	Detail
Source IP Address	Field requires IPv4 or IPv6 address of the Source
Fully Qualified Domain Name of Source IP	Field Requires Fully Qualified Domain name, this is the mandatory field. It does not attempt to reverse DNS Lookup to check if IP address matches to the FQDN but if it is not provided, it attempt reverse DNS lookup to get FQDN.
Listener to Trace Behaviour on	Select from the list of listeners configured on the ESA to emulate the test message
SenderBase Network Owner Organization ID	Field requires Unique Identification number of SenderBase network owner. You can simply allow the device to lookup network owner ID associated with Source IP address
SenderBase Reputation Score (SBRS Score)	Filed requires SBRS score for spoofed domain. You can simply allow to lookup the SBRS score associated with Source IP address
Envelope Sender	Type the Envelope Sender of the test message.
Envelope Recipients	Type a list of recipients for the test message. Separate multiple entries with commas.
Message Body	Content of the Message

Table 5-02: ESA Trace Tool Inputs

ESA Reporting

Reporting Overview

Reporting function of Cisco Email Security Appliance (ESA) offers three ways for reporting including Scheduled Reports, On-demand Reports and Archived Reports. Scheduled Reports are configured to be run on daily basis, weekly or monthly basis, On-demand reports are the immediate reports created at run time on demand whereas Archived reports are the archived version of these reports.

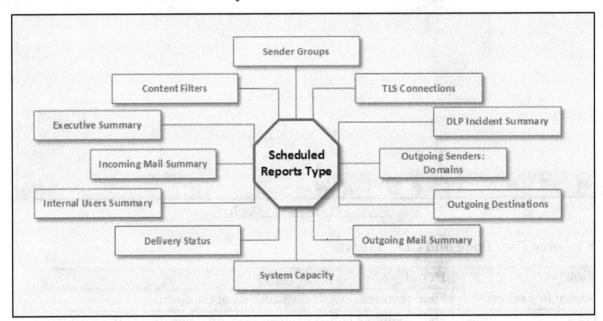

Figure 5-22: ESA Reporting Options

Scheduled Reporting

Following are the steps in order to configure the Scheduling the Report:

1. Go to Monitor > Scheduled Reports, click Add Scheduled Report.

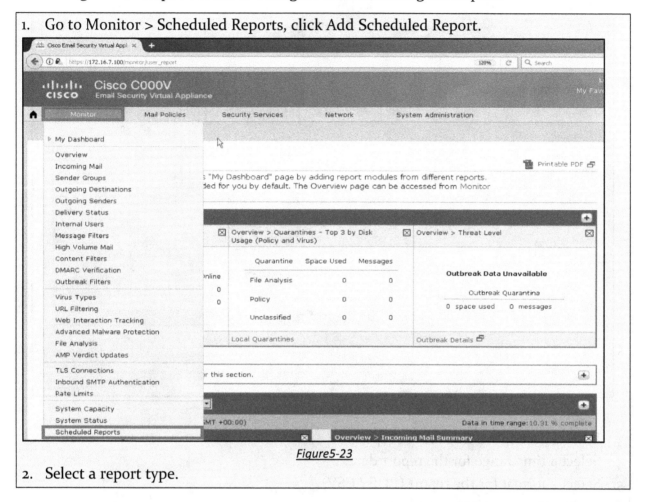

Figure5-23

2. Select a report type.

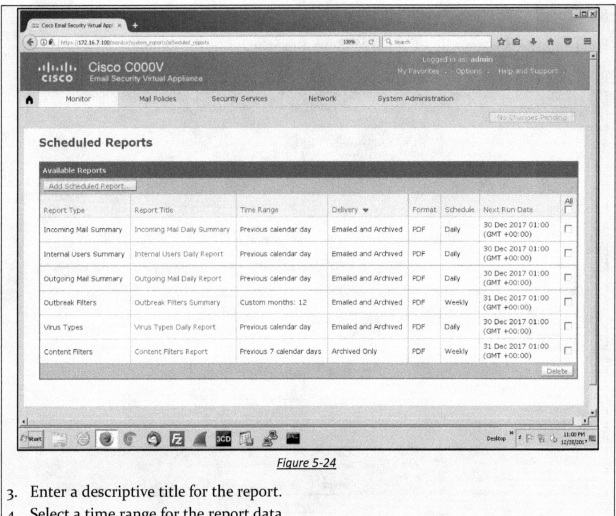

Figure 5-24

3. Enter a descriptive title for the report.

4. Select a time range for the report data.

5. Select a format for the report (PDF / CSV)

6. Specify the report options, if available.

7. Specify scheduling and delivery options.

8. Click Submit. Commit your changes.

Archived Reporting

Archived Report section is available at **Monitor > Archived Reports**. In this section, all archived reports are listed by the names. This page also offers the generation of report immediately by the option "**Generate Report Now**".

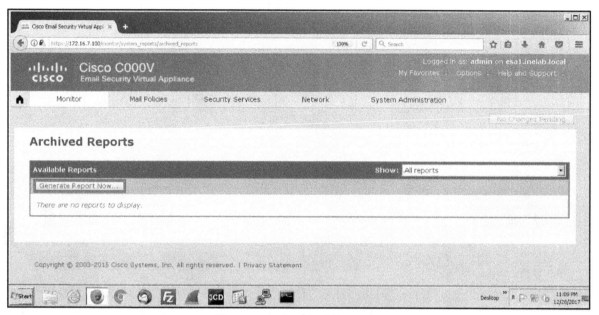

Figure 5-25: Archived Reporting

Archived Report in this section are deleted automatically. Up to 1000 reports can be recorded based on 30 files of each scheduled report. Addition of new report will delete the last report.

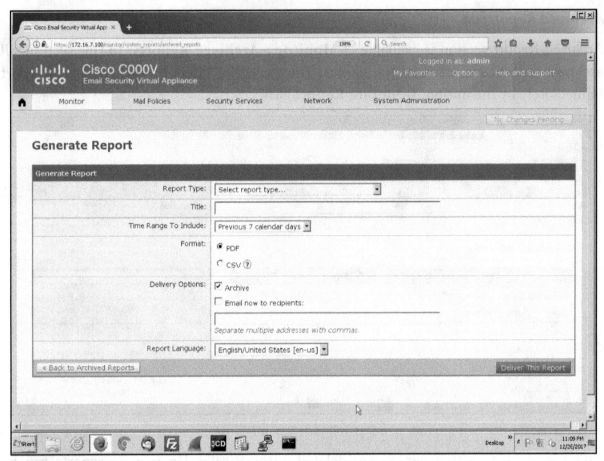

Figure 5-26: Archived Reporting

Troubleshooting Using CLI Tools

There are a number of Command Line Interface Commands which can help in troubleshooting the different issues regarding network connectivity, Email Delivery, Packet flow, and appliance with different aspects. The following are the major issues and associated commands which are helpful when facing any issue that occur during deployment of Email Security Solution with Cisco Email Security Appliance.

Debugging Mail Flow

In an Email Security Solution, you can trace the Email flow by using Trace feature form CLI. The purpose and result are the same as defined in ESA policy Trace Tool section.

Troubleshooting Appliance

To test the appliance and message generation system, black hole listeners are configured to inspect the message generation and a measure of performance of receiving of message. Black hole listeners are either queueing or non-queueing. Queueing black hole listener first save the message in the queue and then delete which helps in troubleshooting and monitoring the performance of the injection whereas Non-Queueing listeners delete the

message immediately. Non-Queueing listener are configured to troubleshoot the connection in between message generation system to ESA.

Command Syntax: **Listenerconfig**

```
WSA                                                    —    □    ×

ironport.example.com> listenerconfig
Currently configured listeners:
1. InboundMail (on PublicNet, 10.10.50.1) SMTP Port 25 Public
2. OutboundMail (on PrivateNet, 192.168.10.1) SMTP Port 25 Private
Choose the operation you want to perform:
 NEW - Create a new listener.
 EDIT - Modify a listener.
 DELETE - Remove a listener.
 SETUP - Change global settings.
[]> new
```

Figure 5-27: Configuring Black Hole Listener

```
WSA                                                    —    □    ×

Please select the type of listener you want to create.
1. Private
2. Public
3. Blackhole
[2]> 3

Do you want messages to be queued onto disk? [N]> y
Please create a name for this listener (Ex: "OutboundMail"):
[]> BlackHole_1
```

Figure 5-28: Configuring Black Hole Listener

Once you configured black hole queuing listener, modify the HAT to accept the connections from your injection system. From Message Generation system, start sending email to the appliance. Use the status, status detail, and rate commands to monitor system performance or monitor the system via the Graphical User Interface (GUI).

Troubleshooting Network

- Command Syntax: **netstat**

  The command "***netstat***" is used to display the routing tables of incoming and outgoing network connections, Network Interfaces statistics along with the List of active Sockets, State of network interfaces, Content of routing table, Size of listen queues & packet traffic information.

- Command Syntax: **diagnostic**

The command "*diagnostic*" can be used to flush the network caches as well as for viewing System ARP cache.

- Command Syntax: **packetcapture**

The command "*packetcapture*" can be used to display and intercept TCP/IP packets transmitted or received across the network.

- Command Syntax: **ping**

The command "*ping*" can be used to ensure the active connection to the network host from appliance.

- Command Syntax: **traceroute**

The command "*traceroute*" can be used to ensure the connectivity to the network host from appliance. It also displays the summary in hop by hop connectivity result.

- Command Syntax: **nslookup**

The command "*nslookup*" can be used to verify the DNS server.

- Command Syntax: **tophost**

The command "*tophost*" can be used to check list of top 20 host in the queue. This command help in troubleshooting if the issue is associated to particular host or the group of hosts.

Troubleshooting Performance

Commands	Description
rate	Real-time Email operation Monitoring
hostrate	Real-time host Monitoring
status	Check for degradation
statusdetail	Check RAM utilization

Table 5-03: Performance related Commands

Cisco FirePOWER

Cisco FirePOWER Management Center Dashboard

Cisco Firepower Management Center dashboards available on Firepower Management Center and 7000 & 8000 Series devices is a high performance, complex, and customizable monitoring feature which provide brief & exhaustive data like current system status, information about the events triggered and collected by the system. Management Center dashboards also show status information and overall health of the appliances in your deployment scenario. All information showing on the dashboard of FirePOWER devices are associated to the configuration of appliance and depends on how you license.

Firepower System Dashboard Widgets

FirePOWER System dashboard has more than one tab associated with the predefined dashboard widgets. The Firepower System delivered these predefined dashboard widgets, providing information to look insight with different aspects. Widgets are grouped into three categories:

- *Analysis & Reporting widgets*
  Analysis and Reporting widgets provide data regarding events collected and generated by the Firepower System.

- *Operations widgets*
  Operations widgets provide status information and overall health of the Firepower System.

- *Miscellaneous widgets*
  Miscellaneous widgets provide an RSS feed.

Dashboard Widget Availability by User Role

The FirePOWER Management Center Dashboard widgets are available for users according to their roles. The table below contains the list of the Dashboard widgets associated to the user account privileges. Required user accounts are Administrator, Maintenance User, Security Analyst, or Security Analyst (Read Only) accounts. Similarly, user defined with customized roles have access of widget, or no access to dashboard widgets according to the roles.

The dashboard widgets a privileged user can view depend upon:

- Type of appliance
- User role
- Current domain (in a multi-domain deployment)

Widget	Admin	Maintenance User	Security Analyst	Security Analyst (RO)
Appliance Information	yes	yes	yes	yes
Appliance Status	yes	yes	yes	no
Correlation Events	yes	no	yes	yes
Current Interface Status	yes	yes	yes	yes
Current Sessions	yes	no	no	no
Custom Analysis	yes	no	yes	yes
Disk Usage	yes	yes	yes	yes
Interface Traffic	yes	yes	yes	yes
Intrusion Events	yes	no	yes	yes
Network Compliance	yes	no	yes	yes
Product Licensing	yes	yes	no	no
Product Updates	yes	yes	no	no
RSS Feed	yes	yes	yes	yes
System Load	yes	yes	yes	yes
System Time	yes	yes	yes	yes
White List Events	yes	no	yes	yes

Table 5-04: Widget availability based on User Role

Health Policy

Health policy requires configured criteria for health test for several modules. Through health policy, health module can be associated against appliance. In can of multiple health module, each can be associated against multiple appliances. While configuring a health policy, you can enable health module for that policy. It offers selection of criteria controlling which health status of enabled module reports. Health policy can also be applied on every appliance across your system. You can customize health policy for specific appliance with respect to the required responses as well as you can use Default health policy to apply on the appliance.

Default Health Policy

In Order to configure quick health monitoring, the health monitor offers default health policy which provide quick and easy implementation of Health monitoring. Default health Policy provide automatically enabled most of the health monitoring modules, this default health policy cannot be edited but it offers the copy option to copy the default Health policy to another customized health monitoring policy for further modification. Default health Policy is automatically enabled for FirePOWER Management Center but you enable it for managed devices.

Steps to Configure Health Monitoring Policy

1. Choose **System > Health > Policy.**

Figure 5-29

2. Click **Create Policy**.

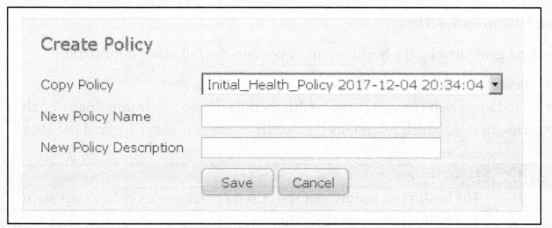

Figure 5-30

3. Choose the existing policy, you want to copy and edit.
4. Enter a name for the policy.
5. Enter a description for the policy.
6. Choose **Save** to save the policy information.
7. Choose the module you want to use.
8. Choose **On** for the **Enabled** option to enable use of the module for health status testing.

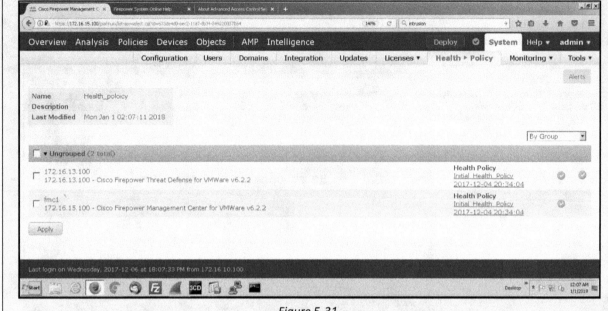

Figure 5-31

9. To save your changes to this module and return to the **Health Policy** page, click **Save Policy** and Exit.

Health Monitoring Alerts

The alerts generated by the health monitor contain the following information:

- Severity, which represents the severity level of the alert.
- Module, which represents the health module whose test results triggered the alert.
- Description, which represents the health test results that triggered the alert.

Severity	Description
Critical	The health test results met the criteria to trigger a Critical alert status.
Warning	The health test results met the criteria to trigger a Warning alert status.
Normal	The health test results met the criteria to trigger a Normal alert status.
Error	The health test did not run.
Recovered	The health test results met the criteria to return to a normal alert status, following a Critical or Warning alert status.

Table 5-05: Health Monitoring Alerts

Health Monitor

The health monitor offers health status for all devices that are managed by the Firepower Management Center. The health monitor is composed of:

- ### Status Table

Provides count of the managed appliances for this Firepower Management Center by overall health status.

- ### Pie chart

Indicates the percentage of appliances currently in each health status category.

- ### Appliance list

Provides details on the health of the managed devices.

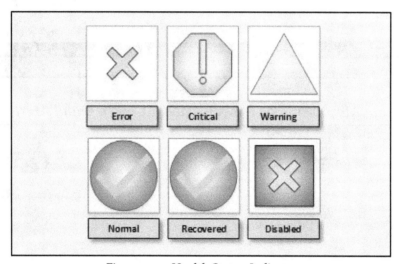

Figure 5-32: Health Status Indicator

Configuring Email Alerts

1. Choose *Policies > Actions > Alerts.*

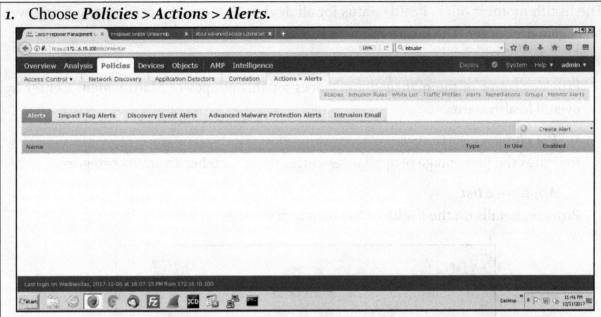

Figure 5-33

2. From the *Create Alert* drop-down menu, choose *Create Email Alert*.

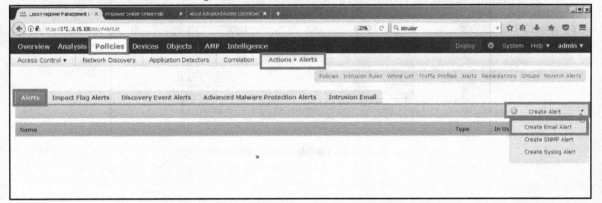

Figure 5-34

3. Enter a Name for the alert response.

4. In the *To* field, enter the email addresses where you want to send alerts, separated by commas.

5. In the from field, enter the email address that you want to appear as the sender of the alert.

6. Next to Relay Host, verify the listed mail server is the one that you want to use to send the alert.

7. To change the email server, click the edit icon.

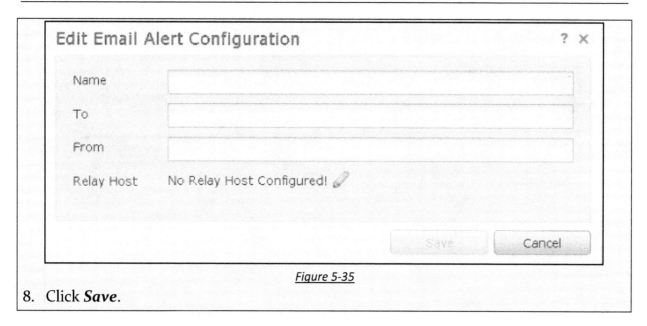

Figure 5-35

8. Click **Save**.

Configuring SNMP Alerts

1. Choose **Policies** > **Actions** > **Alerts.**

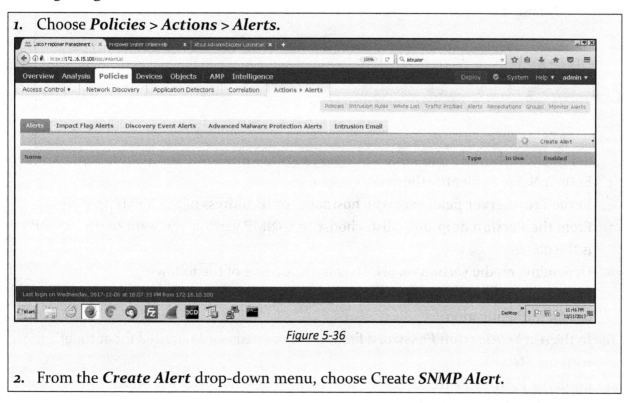

Figure 5-36

2. From the **Create Alert** drop-down menu, choose Create **SNMP Alert.**

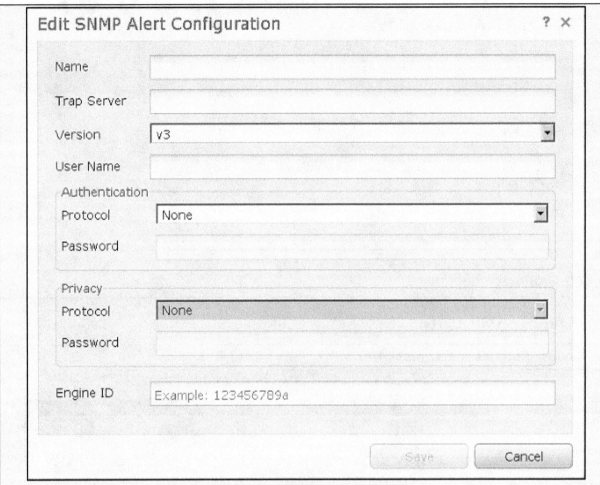

Figure 5-37

3. Enter a Name to identify the SNMP response.

4. In the **Trap Server** field, enter the hostname or IP address of the SNMP trap server.

5. From the **Version** drop-down list, choose the SNMP version you want to use. SNMP v3 is the default.

6. Depending on the version on SNMP you use, do one of the following:

7. From the **Authentication Protocol** drop-down list, choose the protocol you want to use for authentication.

8. In the **Authentication Password** field, enter the password required for authentication with the SNMP server.

9. From the **Privacy Protocol** list, choose None to use no privacy protocol or DES to use Data Encryption Standard as the privacy protocol.

10. In the **Privacy Password** field, enter the privacy password required by the SNMP server.

11. In the **Engine ID** field, enter an identifier for the SNMP engine, in hexadecimal notation, using an even number of digits.

12. Click **Save**

Configuring Syslog Alerts

1. In the intrusion policy editor's navigation pane, click **Advanced Settings**.
2. Make sure **Syslog Alerting** is **Enabled**, then click **Edit**.
3. Enter the IP addresses of the **Logging Hosts** where you want to send syslog alerts.
4. Choose **Facility and Priority levels**
5. To save changes you made in this policy since the last policy commit, choose **Policy Information**, then click **Commit Changes**.
6. If you leave the policy without committing changes, changes since the last commit are discarded if you edit a different policy.

Troubleshooting NGIPS Using CLI Tools

In the FirePOWER devices including NGIPS, there are numerous CLI modes. In these mode, commands are associated to users according to their associated user access level. These mode includes several modes such as show mode, configure mode & System mode. These modes contain several of commands which begin with the mode name.

Basically, to issue a command you have to enter mode name and associated command and other associated parameters along with it. For example,

```
[Mode][Command][Option]
show user [Username]
```

If you have already in show mode, enter the following at the CLI prompt:

```
user [Username]
```

```
registration key is always required.  In most cases, to register a sensor
to a Defense Center, you must provide the hostname or the IP address along
with the registration key.
'configure manager add [hostname | ip address ] [registration key ]'

However, if the sensor and the Defense Center are separated by a NAT device,
you must enter a unique NAT ID, along with the unique registration key.
'configure manager add DONTRESOLVE [registration key ] [ NAT ID ]'

Later, using the web interface on the Defense Center, you must use the same
registration key and, if necessary, the same NAT ID when you add this
sensor to the Defense Center.
>

configure   Change to Configuration mode
end         Return to the default mode
exit        Exit this CLI session
expert      Invoke a shell
help        Display an overview of the CLI syntax
history     Display the current session's command line history
logout      Logout of the current CLI session
show        Change to Show Mode
system      Change to System Mode
>
```

Figure 5-38: NGIPS CLI Options

Command Line Interface (CLI) Access Level

Each mode of Command line, commands are accessible to a user according to the user's CLI access levels. You can configure User access level while creating a user account. There are 3 type of CLI access levels which can be assigned:

CLI Access Level	Description
Basic	The user has read-only access and cannot run commands that impact system performance.
Configuration	The user has read-write access and can run commands that impact system performance.
None	The user is unable to log in to the shell.

Table 5-06: NGIPS CLI Access Levels

7000 and 8000 Series FirePOWER devices, you can assign command line permissions on the User Management page in the web interface. On NGIPSv and ASA FirePOWER, you assign command line permissions using the CLI.

Basic CLI access Level Commands

Command Syntax	Description
?	Displays context-sensitive help for CLI commands and parameters.
??	Displays detailed context-sensitive help for CLI commands and parameters.
configure password	Allows the current user to change their password.
help	Displays an overview of the CLI syntax.
history [limit]	Displays the command line history for the current session.
logout	Logs the current user out of the current CLI console session.
end	Returns the user to the default mode
exit	Moves the CLI context up to the next highest CLI context level

Table 5-07: NGIPS Basic Commands

CLI Troubleshooting Commands

Syntax	Description
show access-control-config	Displays current access control configurations.
show audit-log	Displays the audit log in reverse chronological order; the most recent audit log events are listed first.
show audit_cert	Displays the current audit log client certificate.
show high-availability config	Displays the high-availability configuration on the device.
show high-availability ha-statistics	Displays state sharing statistics for a device in a high-availability pair.
show cpu	Displays the current CPU usage statistics
show database processes	Displays a list of running database queries.
show database slow-query-log	Displays the slow query log of the database.
show device-settings	Displays information about application bypass settings specific to the current device.
show disk	Displays the current disk usage.
show disk-manager	Displays detailed disk usage information for each part of the system.
show dns	Displays the current DNS server addresses and search domains.
show hostname	Displays the device's host name and appliance UUID.
show hyperthreading	Displays whether hyperthreading is enabled or disabled.

show inline-sets	Displays configuration data for all inline security zones and associated interfaces.
show interfaces	Displays detailed information about the specified interface.
show link-aggregation statistics	Displays statistics, per interface, for each configured LAG.
show link-state	Displays type, link, speed, duplex state, and bypass mode of the ports on the device
show log-ips-connection	Displays whether the logging of connection events that are associated with logged intrusion events is enabled or disabled.
show managers	Displays the configuration and communication status of the Firepower Management Center.
show memory	Displays the total memory, the memory in use, and the available memory for the device.
show model	Displays model information for the device.
show network	Display management Interface information.
show network-static-routes	Displays all configured network static routes and information.
show ntp	Displays the ntp configuration.
show perfstats	Displays performance statistics for the device.
show process-tree	Displays processes currently running on the device, sorted in tree format by type.
show ssl-policy-config	Displays the currently deployed SSL policy configuration.
show stacking	Shows the stacking configuration and position on managed devices.
show summary	Displays a summary of the most commonly used information.
show syslog	Displays the system log in reverse chronological order.
show time	Displays the current date and time in UTC and in the local time zone.
show traffic-statistics [port]	Display traffic information for Specified port.
show version [detail]	Display Product Version information.
show virtual-routers [dhcprelay	ospf	rip] [name]	Show Virtual Router Information.
show virtual-switches [name]	Display information of Virtual Switch.
show vmware-tools	Indicate VMware tool is enabled or disabled.
show vpn config	Displays the configuration of all VPN connections.
show vpn status	Displays the status of all VPN connections.

Table 5-08: NGIPS Troubleshooting Commands

References

- https://www.cisco.com
- https://msdn.microsoft.com
- www.intel.com
- https://www.snort.org
- https://meraki.cisco.com
- http://www.cisco.com/c/en/us/td/docs/solutions/Enterprise/Campus/campover.html#wp7141
- https://blogs.cisco.com/ take-incident-response-to-the-next-level-with-amp-for-endpoints
- https://docs.amp.cisco.com/en/A4/AMP%20for%20Endpoints%20Quick%20Start.pdf
- https://www.cisco.com/c/en/us/products/collateral/security/whitepaper_c73277.pdf
- https://blogs.cisco.com/security/security-beyond-the-sandbox
- https://www.cisco.com/c/en/us/td/docs/security/firepower/configuration/guide/fpmc-config-guide-v60/Detecting_Specific_Threats.html
- https://www.cisco.com/c/en/us/td/docs/security/firesight/541/user-guide/FireSIGHT-System-UserGuide-v540/NAP-Transport-Network-Layer.pdf
- https://www.cisco.com/c/dam/en/us/docs/security/content_security/virtual_appliances/Cisco_Content_Security_Virtual_Appliance_Install_Guide.pdf
- https://www.cisco.com/c/dam/en/us/td/docs/security/content_security/virtual_appliances/Content_Security_Config_Migration_1-0_Release_Notes.pdf
- https://www.cisco.com/c/en/us/products/collateral/security/email-security-appliance/data-sheet-c78-729751.pdf
- https://www.cisco.com/c/dam/en/us/products/collateral/security/hybrid-email-security/hybrid_benefits_datasheet.pdf
- https://www.cisco.com/c/en/us/support/security/hybrid-email-security/model.html
- https://www.cisco.com/c/en/us/td/docs/security/firepower/60/configuration/guide/fpmc-config-guide-v60/Setting_Up_Virtual_Switches.html#ID-2266-00000058
- http://www.cisco.com/c/en/us/td/docs/solutions/Enterprise/Campus/campover.html#wp7141
- http://www.cisco.com/web/services/downloads/smart-solutions-maximize-federal-capabilities-for-mission-success.pdf
- http://www.cisco.com/c/en/us/support/docs/availability/high-availability/15114-NMS-bestpractice.html
- http://www.ciscopress.com/articles/article.asp?p=2180210&seqNum=5
- http://www.cisco.com/c/en/us/td/docs/wireless/prime_infrastructure/1-3/configuration/guide/pi_13_cg/ovr.pdf
- http://www.cisco.com/c/en/us/products/security/security-manager/index.html
- http://www.cisco.com/c/en/us/about/security-center/dnssec-best-practices.html
- http://www.cisco.com/c/en/us/td/docs/ios-xml/ios/sec_usr_ssh/configuration/15-s/sec-usr-ssh-15-s-book/sec-secure-copy.html
- http://www.ciscopress.com/articles/article.asp?p=25477&seqNum=3
- http://www.cisco.com/c/en/us/products/security/ids-4215-sensor/index.html

About Our Products

Other Network & Security related products from IPSpecialist LTD are:

- CCNA Routing & Switching Technology Workbook
- CCNA Security v2 Technology Workbook
- CCNA Service Provider Technology Workbook
- CCDA Technology Workbook
- CCDP Technology Workbook
- CCNP Route Technology Workbook
- CCNP Switch Technology Workbook
- CCNP Troubleshoot Technology Workbook
- CCNP Security SENSS Technology Workbook
- CCNP Security SITCS Technology Workbook
- CCNP Security SISAS Technology Workbook
- CompTIA Network+ Technology Workbook
- CompTIA Security+ v2 Technology Workbook
- Certified Information System Security Professional (CISSP) Technology Workbook
- CCNA CyberOps SECFND Technology Workbook
- Certified Block Chain Expert Technology Workbook
- Certified Cloud Security Professional (CCSP) Technology Workbook
- CompTIA Pentest+ Technology Workbook

Upcoming products are:

- CompTIA A+ Core 1 (220-1001) Technology Workbook
- CompTIA A+ Core 2 (220-1002) Technology Workbook
- CompTIA Cyber Security Analyst CySA+ Technology Workbook
- CompTIA Cloud+ Technology Workbook
- CompTIA Server+ Technology Workbook